s Poetry

Everyman, I will go with thee,
and be thy guide

W. B. Yeats

Selected and edited by JOHN KELLY

University of Oxford

EVERYMAN
J. M. Dent · London

This edition first published by Everyman Paperbacks in 1997
Selection, introduction and other critical apparatus
© J.M.Dent 1997

Reprinted 1998, 1999, 2000, 2001

J.M.Dent
Orion Publishing Group
Orion House
5 Upper St Martin's Lane,
London WC2H 9EA

Typeset by Deltatype Ltd, Birkenhead, Merseyside
Printed in Great Britain by
The Guernsey Press Co. Ltd, Guernsey, C.I.

British Library Cataloguing-in-Publication
Data is available on request.

ISBN 0 460 87902 2

Contents

from In the Seven Woods (1904)

from The Green Helmet and Other Poems (1910)

from Responsibilities (1914)

from The Wild Swans at Coole (1919)

from Michael Robartes and the Dancer (1921)

from The Tower (1928)

from A Man Young and Old (1927)

from The Winding Stair and Other Poems (1933)

from Words for Music Perhaps

from A Woman Young and Old

from A Full Moon In March (1935)

from Supernatural Songs

from New Poems (1938)

from On the Boiler (1938)

Note on the Author and Editor

WILLIAM BUTLER YEATS was born on 13 June 1865 in Dublin, the eldest of six children, two of whom died in infancy. His father, John Butler Yeats, abandoned a career in the law for a precarious life as a painter, and much of Yeats's childhood was divided between Dublin, London, and Sligo, for which he had a particular love. His meeting with John O'Leary and Standish O'Grady in the mid-1880s helped convince him that he should choose Irish themes for his poetry, and he was soon active in setting up cultural organizations which laid the foundation for the 'Irish Literary Revival'. His early poetry draws inspiration from his unrequited love for Maud Gonne, the beautiful and politically active woman he met in 1889, from Irish folklore, his occult studies, and contemporary ideas on Celticism. In 1897 he helped found the Irish Literary Theatre, which gave its first productions in 1899, and which was to lead to the Abbey Theatre in 1904. Writing for the stage changed Yeats's poetry: his style became more dramatic, more sinewy, and more colloquial, while his themes show an increasing disillusionment with the modern world. The experience of the First World War and the Anglo-Irish and Irish Civil Wars intensified these feelings, and many of the poems of his 'middle period' are impassioned meditations on historical and personal decline and on poetic responsibility. In 1917 Yeats married Georgie Hyde-Lees, whose automatic writing was the basis for his 'philosophy', as adumbrated in *A Vision*, and who bore him two children. In 1922 he was appointed to the new Irish Senate, and the following year he won the Nobel Prize. Illness in his later years caused him to spend winters abroad, and he died at Mentone in the South of France in January 1939, still writing poetry on his deathbed.

JOHN KELLY is Professor of English and Senior English Fellow at St. John's College, Oxford. He is General Editor of *The Collected Letters of W. B. Yeats*, being published in 12 volumes, and has written widely on Modern and Anglo-Irish literature.

Chronology of Yeats's Life

Year	Age	Life
1865		13 June, born Sandymount Avenue, Dublin
1866		25 August, birth of sister, Susan Mary (Lily)
1867	1	Early March, father abandons law and moves to art school in London; family join him in late July
1868	2	11 March, birth of sister, Elizabeth Corbet (Lollie)
1870	4	27 March, birth of brother, Robert Corbet (Bobbie)
1871	6	29 August, birth of brother, John Butler (Jack)
1872	7	23 July, mother and children move to Sligo
1874	9	October, family rejoin father in London
1875	10	29 August, birth of sister Jane Grace
1879	13	Spring, moves with family to Bedford Park, London
1881	16	Autumn, moves with family to Howth, Dublin, and enrolled in Dublin High School
1884	18	Enrolls in Metropolitan School of Art, Dublin
1885	19	Spring, meets the Fenian John O'Leary
		March, first poems published
1886	20	April, leaves Metropolitan School of Art
	21	June, *Mosada*, his first book, privately printed
	22	August, in Sligo and, in November, Dublin
1888	23	September, *Fairy and Folk Tales of the Irish Peasantry*
1889	23	January, *The Wanderings of Oisin*, first book of poems
		30 January, first meeting with Maud Gonne
	24	23 August, his edition of *Stories from Carleton*
1890	24	11 January, founds the Rhymers' Club with Rhys
		7 March, initiated into the Order of the Golden Dawn

Chronology of his Times

Year	Cultural Context	Historical Events
1865	Swinburne, *Atalanta in Calydon*	Death of Palmerston End of American Civil War
1866	Eliot, *Felix Holt*	Gladstone's Reform Bill defeated
1867	Marx, *Das Kapital*	Fenian Rising 'Manchester Martyrs' executed
1868		Gladstone's first Ministry
1870	Rossetti, *Poems*	Gladstone's first Irish Land Act
1871	Darwin, *The Descent of Man*	Local Government Act
1874		Disraeli becomes Prime Minister
1875	Tolstoy, *Anna Karenina*	
1879	Ibsen, *A Doll's House*	Davitt founds the Land League
1881	Ibsen, *Ghosts* Wilde, *Poems*	Gladstone's second Land Act
1884	Huysmans, *A Rebours* Ibsen, *The Wild Duck*	Third Reform Act extends franchise to agricultural labourers
1885	Pater, *Marius the Epicurean*	Alliance between Gladstone and Irish Party
1886	Nietzsche, *Ideas of Good and Evil*	Gladstone's first Home Rule Bill defeated
1888	Kipling, *Plain Tales from the Hills*	Commission to examine allegations against Parnell
1889	Death of Browning Symons, *Days and Nights*	Suicide of Crown Prince Rudolph of Austria
1890	Frazer, *The Golden Bough*	Parnell cited in the O'Shea divorce suit

Year	Age	Life
1891	25	March, his edition of *Representative Irish Tales*
	26	November, stories *John Sherman and Dhoya*
1892	26	February, *The Book of the Rhymers' Club*
		May, anthology *Irish Fairy Tales*
		16 August, helps inaugurate National Literary Society
	27	Late August, *The Countess Kathleen and Various Legends and Lyrics*
1893	27	20 January, initiated into Second Order of Golden Dawn
	28	November, *The Poems of William Blake*
		December, *The Celtic Twilight*
1894	28	February, first visit to Paris; calls on Maud Gonne, meets Verlaine, and sees Villiers de l'Isle-Adam's *Axel*
		March and April, *The Land of Heart's Desire* in London
	29	June, *The Second Book of the Rhymers' Club*
1895	29	March, *A Book of Irish Verse*
		19 May, offers Wilde support during his trial
	30	October, takes rooms with Symons in the Temple
1896	30	February, moves to own rooms at 18 Woburn Buildings
		Consummates his affair with Olivia Shakespear
	31	25 July, in Ireland with Symons until October
		5–7 August, visits the Aran Islands
		December, in Paris; sees Jarry's *Ubu Roi*; meets Synge
		23 December, signs agreement for the never-completed novel *The Speckled Bird*
1897	31	16 February, elected Chairman of the London '98 Centennial
	32	July, first of many extended visits to Lady Gregory at Coole Park, Galway
1899	33	January, in Paris to propose to Maud Gonne
		15 April, *The Wind among the Reeds*
		8 May, *Poems* (1899), and first productions of Irish Literary Theatre (ILT)
1900	34	3 January, mother dies in London
		Publicly denounces Queen Victoria's visit to Ireland

Year	Cultural Context	Historical Events
1891	Wilde, *The Picture of Dorian Gray*	7 October, Death of Parnell
1892	Death of Tennyson Maeterlinck, *Pelléas et Mélisande* Kipling, *Barrack Room Ballads*	Gladstone's second Home Rule Bill defeated
1893	Gaelic League founded Wilde, *Salome*	
1894	Moore, *Esther Waters* Shaw, *Candida*	Gladstone retires
1895	Wilde, *The Importance of Being Ernest*	Conservatives' policy of 'killing Home Rule with kindness'
1896	Deaths of Morris and Verlaine	The Jameson Raid fails in South Africa
1897	Havelock Ellis, *Studies in the Psychology of Sex* AE, *The Earth Breath*	Queen Victoria's Diamond Jubilee
1899	Symons, *The Symbolist Movement in Literature*	The Boer War begins Local Government Act alters political power in Ireland
1900	Freud, *The Interpretation of Dreams*	Reunification of the Irish Party under Redmond Relief of Mafeking

Year	Age	Life
1901	35	January, contributes to *Ideals in Ireland*
	36	21–2 October, *Diarmuid and Grania*
1902	36	April, Fay brothers produce *Cathleen ni Houlihan*
	37	October, first Irish National Theatre (INT) productions, including *The Pot of Broth*
1903	37	21 February, Maud Gonne marries John MacBride
		May, *Ideas of Good and Evil*
	38	August, *In the Seven Woods*
		11 November, begins lecturing tour of USA
1904	39	29 June, meets Queen Alexandria in London
		27 December, first productions at Abbey Theatre
1905	40	8 July, London production of *The Shadowy Waters*
1906	41	September, *The Poems of Spenser*
		October, *Poems 1899–1905*
1907	41	January, riots at Abbey Theatre over Synge's *The Playboy of the Western World*
	42	December, *Discoveries*
		21 December, father moves to New York
1908		November, Mrs Pat Campbell plays *Deirdre* in Dublin and London
1909	43	24 March, Synge dies
1910	44	May, stays with Maud Gonne in Normandy
	45	9 August, granted Civil List pension of £150 p.a.
		December, *The Green Helmet and Other Poems*
1911	46	26 July, *Synge and the Ireland of His Time*
		September, accompanies Abbey Players to USA
1912	47	June, meets Tagore
		13 November, *The Cutting of an Agate*
1913	47	Summer, experiments with automatic writing
	48	October, *Poems Written in Discouragement*
		November, rents cottage in Sussex with Ezra Pound, and winters there for following four years
1914	48	January to April, American tour
		25 May, *Responsibilities*
1915	49	May, Hugh Lane drowned on the *Lusitania*
	50	December, refuses a knighthood

Year	Cultural Context	Historical Events
1901	Rhys, *Celtic Folklore* Kipling, *Kim*	Death of Queen of Victoria and accession of Edward VII
1902	Death of Lionel Johnson Lady Gregory, *Cuchulain of Muirthemne*	Balfour succeeds Lord Salisbury as Prime Minister End of the Boer War
1903	Shaw, *Man and Superman* Synge, *In the Shadow of the Glen*	Wyndham's Land Act settles Irish Land question
1904	Conrad, *Nostromo*	Roosevelt re-elected US President
1905	Synge, *The Well of the Saints*	Liberal government under Campbell Bannerman
1906	De la Mare, *Poems*	Liberals, supported by Irish Party, re-elected
1907	Synge, *The Playboy of the Western World* Shaw, *John Bull's Other Island* Gosse, *Father and Son*	Russia joins Anglo-French alliance
1908	Forster, *A Room with a View*	Irish National University founded Asquith becomes Prime Minister
1909	Death Swinburne	Bleriot flies the English channel
1910	Deaths of Twain and Tolstoy	December, Irish Party holds balance of power at Westminster
1911	Moore, *Ave* Pound, *Canzoni*	Payment of MPs introduced
1912	Moore, *Salve*	Third Home Rule Bill introduced
1913	Lawrence, *Sons and Lovers* Proust, *À la Recherche du Temps Perdu*	January, Home Rule Bill defeated in House of Lords Ulster and National Volunteers founded
1914	Joyce, *Dubliners* Moore, *Vale*	March, the 'Curragh Mutiny' Third Home Rule Bill suspended
1915	Pound, *Cathay* Lawrence, *The Rainbow*	*Lusitania* torpedoed

Year	Age	Life
1916	50	20 March, *Reveries over Childhood and Youth*
		4 April, *At the Hawk's Well*, his first Noh play, produced
	51	July, asks Maud Gonne to marry him
1917	51	March, buys Tower at Ballylee
	52	August, proposes to Iseult Gonne but is refused
		20 October, marries George Hyde-Lees
		On honeymoon wife begins automatic writing that becomes basis of *A Vision*
		17 November, *The Wild Swans at Coole*
1918	52	January, moves to Oxford
		18 January, *Per Amica Silentia Lunae*
1919	53	January, *Two Plays for Dancers*
		26 February, daughter Anne born
		9 May, family returns to England
		25 May, *The Player Queen*
	54	October, family moves to 4 Broad Street, Oxford
1920	54	January to May, lectures in USA
1921	55	February, *Michael Robartes and the Dancer*
		17 February, denounces British policy in Ireland at Oxford Union
	56	22 August, son Michael born
		28 October, *Four Plays for Dancers*
		December, *Four Years*
1922	56	3 February, father dies in New York
		20 March, family moves from Oxford to Dublin
	57	October, *The Trembling of the Veil*
		11 December, appointed Senator of the Irish Free State
1923	58	November, awarded the Nobel Prize
		27 November, *Plays and Controversies*
1924	58	6 May, *Essays*
1926	60	15 January, *A Vision*
	61	5 November, *Autobiographies*
1927	62	November, seriously ill with congestion of the lungs

Year	Cultural Context	Historical Events
1916	Joyce, *Portrait of the Artist as a Young Man* Moore, *The Brook Kerith*	Easter Rising in Dublin Execution of Sir Roger Casement for treason Lloyd George Prime Minister
1917	Eliot, *Prufrock* Edward Thomas, *Poems* Valéry, *La Jeune Parque*	February, Sinn Fein wins Roscommon by-election Battles of Messines, Passchendaele, Cambrai USA declares war on Germany Russian Revolution
1918	Joyce, *Exiles* Hopkins, *Poems*	Sinn Fein wins resounding election victory
1919	Shaw, *Heartbreak House* Eliot, *Poems*	January, Sinn Fein deputies proclaim Irish Republic Beginning of Anglo-Irish guerilla war
1920	Pound, *Hugh Selwyn Mauberley*	Use of Black and Tans intensifies war in Ireland
1921	Huxley, *Chrome Yellow* Shaw, *Back to Methuselah*	22 June, King opens Northern Irish parliament 6 December, Anglo-Irish Treaty signed in London
1922	Joyce, *Ulysses* Eliot, *The Waste Land* Mansfield, *The Garden Party*	7 January, ratification of Treaty by Dáil Eireann leads to Irish Civil War Resignation of Lloyd George Assassination of Michael Collins
1923	O'Casey, *The Shadow of a Gunman*	Irish Civil War ends August, Irish general election
1924	Shaw, *St Joan*	First British Labour Government
1926	O'Casey, *The Plough and the Stars*	de Valera secedes from Sinn Fein to found Fianna Fáil
1927	Woolf, *To the Lighthouse*	July, O'Higgins, Irish Minister for Justice, assassinated

Year	Age	Life
1928	62	14 February, *The Tower*
		June, controversy over Abbey's rejection of O'Casey's *The Silver Tassie*
	63	31 July, moves to 42 Fitzwilliam Square, Dublin
		September, resigns Senate seat
1929	64	December, dangerously ill with Malta fever
1930	65	Slow convalescence at Rapallo throughout spring
		July, return to Dublin
1932	66	May, Lady Gregory dies at Coole
	67	July, moves to last Irish home in Rathfarnham, Dublin
		September, helps found Irish Academy of Letters
1933	68	July and August, involved in Irish Blue Shirt movement
		September, *The Winding Stair and Other Poems*
		November, *Collected Poems*
1934	68	April, has Steinach operation in London
		November, *Wheels and Butterflies* and *Collected Plays*
1935	69	Spring, seriously ill with congestion of lungs
	70	June, Dublin celebrations for his 70th birthday
		November, *A Full Moon In March*
		Dramatis Personae published in December
1936	70	January, close to death with heart and kidney ailments
	71	November, *Oxford Book of Modern Verse* causes controversy
1937	71	*The Ten Principal Upanishads*
	72	October, revised edition of *A Vision*
		Essays 1931 to 1936 in December
1938	72	*New Poems* in May
	73	First production of *Purgatory* at Abbey causes theological controversy in August
		Yeatses leave for South of France in November
1939	73	Dies in Mentone and buried at Roquebrune
		Last Poems and Two Plays in July
		On the Boiler in September

Year	Cultural Context	Historical Events
1928	Lawrence, *Lady Chatterley's Lover* Waugh, *Decline and Fall* Woolf, *Orlando*	British Reform Act widens women's franchise
1929		Wall Street Crash
1930	Eliot, *Ash Wednesday*	France evacuates the Rhineland
1932	Joyce, *Two Tales of Shem and Shaun* Auden, *The Orators*	February, Fianna Fáil form coalition government Anglo-Irish economic war
1933	Death of Moore Auden, *The Dance of Death*	January, Fianna Fáil win absolute majority in Irish general election
1934	Toynbee, *A Study in History*	Hindenburg dies and Hitler becomes Reichsführer
1935	Death of AE Eliot, *Murder in the Cathedral*	Baldwin replaces Macdonald as British Prime Minister Italy invades Abyssinia
1936	Auden, *Look, Stranger! Poems* Dylan Thomas, *Twenty-Five Poems*	Abdication crisis culminates in December de Valera declares the IRA illegal Spanish Civil War begins
1937	Woolf, *The Years* Stevens, *The Man with the Blue Guitar*	29 December, new 'Constitution of Eire' adopted following acceptance in July referendum
1938	Beckett, *Murphy* Bowen, *The Death of the Heart*	April, Anglo-Irish agreement ends economic war June, election returns Fianna Fáil with overall majority
1939	Joyce, *Finnegans Wake* Eliot, *The Family Reunion*	

Introduction

T. S. Eliot said that Yeats was 'one of those few whose history is the history of their own time, who are a part of the consciousness of an age which cannot be understood without them'. That age was turbulent. Born in 1865, the period of High Victorianism, Yeats died on the eve of the Second World War in 1939. The intervening years had altered the world he had been born into almost beyond recognition, and the external political and historical changes also had their philosophical and psychological consequences. It is part of the greatness of Yeats's poetry that it attempts to bear witness to these emotional and historical forces.

His Victorian inheritance is important in assessing Yeats, and so is his Irishness. From an early age he refused to subscribe to the prevailing Victorian mood of optimism. His grandfather and great-grandfather had been clergymen, but his father, in common with many of his generation, had abandoned his religious beliefs after reading the works of Charles Darwin and the Positivist philosopher Auguste Comte. In his *Autobiographies* Yeats tells us that he was religious by nature, but, deprived by the post-Darwinians Tyndall and Huxley of the faith of his childhood, he turned to create an alternative church out of literature, and particularly out of literature based on folklore, myth and tradition. His religious quest was also to lead him into unorthodoxy, into association with the theosophists and the Rosicrucian Order of the Golden Dawn, and into making a study of spiritualism, astrology, automatic writing, and psychical research. In its more extreme expression this can strike the modern reader as bizarre and even embarrassing, but Yeats was impelled by a serious purpose: he wished in an increasingly sceptical age to find evidence of the soul's survival and a purpose and pattern in what otherwise appeared to be the confusion and absurdity of modern life. And the imagination, especially the poetic imagination, seemed to him the key agency in lighting upon such evidence.

That modern life was confused and absurd he had no doubt. In one of his first review essays he spoke of that 'leprosy of the modern', which he defined as 'tepid emotions and many aims'. He believed that a vital imaginative culture could cure this 'leprosy', and that Ireland, still rooted in a traditional and more passionate way of life, and with a living popular culture in its abundant folklore, could provide the necessary elements for a literary revival that would mark the triumph of imagination and idealism over materialism and scientific abstraction. He was strengthened in this belief by reading the energetic retelling of Irish myths by the historian Standish O'Grady, and in poring over the Irish books he borrowed from the library of John O'Leary, who had been imprisoned and exiled for his Fenian activities, but who returned to Dublin in 1885.

Yet Yeats's Irishness was a complicated and complicating inheritance. He was born into the Protestant middle class, and was keenly aware that class barriers stood between him and the landowning Ascendancy. As a Protestant he was also divided from the Catholic majority of his countrymen not merely by religion, but by the historical attitudes and memories that religious differences had helped produce. History was now about to marginalise his class even further, for a series of political, educational, and social reforms were to transfer the power it had hitherto enjoyed in Ireland to a growing and increasingly self-confident Catholic middle class. Yeat's crisis of identity was deepened by his long periods of residence in London, where his father, an impecunious painter, periodically took the family as he searched for commissions. It was also exacerbated by his sense of genetic inheritance: the Yeatses were fluent and clubbable Dublin professionals; the Pollexfens, his mother's people, taciturn and brooding Sligo merchants. His father announced that by his marriage into the Pollexfens he had 'given a tongue to the sea cliffs'. His son's career proves this boast no idle one, but the union also produced an acute and sometimes anguished awareness of contrary temperamental and emotional forces at war within his psyche, forces which Yeats was to harness to poetic effect. 'We make out of the quarrel with others, rhetoric', he was to write, 'but out of the quarrel with ourselves, poetry'.

Given his sense of psychological, social, religious and political division, Yeats grew up instinctively confronting those perplexities about the stability of the self and questions of identity that were to become part of the Modernist dilemma. He understood the need for the artist to experiment with identities, to adopt masks, in an attempt to do justice to the inner and outer complexities generated by modern life. But he also felt the need for the artist to work within and for his own society, to seek, as he was to put it, Unity of Being through Unity of Culture. And this inevitably led him into politics.

Like all great artists, Yeats was constantly developing as he tested his works against new perceptions forced upon him by public events and amplified emotional experience. Since this development was a continual process, we should beware of forcing his canon into rigorously defined periods, but it is possible to see broad movements in his poetry and thought. The first might be said to extend from the early 1880s, when he began to write, to 1889 when, at the age of twenty-three, he published his first book of verse, *The Wanderings of Oisin and Other Poems*. Many of these poems were later gathered into the section of his *Collected Poems* that he called *Crossways*, choosing this name because in them he felt tht he had 'tried many pathways'. Indeed he had. These poems have Hungarian, Moorish, Arcadian, and Indian, as well as Irish themes and settings, but by the time *The Wanderings of Oisin* appeared he had already resolved that he would become an Irish poet and 'never go for the scenery of a poem to any country but my own'. Under the influence of O'Leary and O'Grady, the long process of finding a Unity of thought and expression had begun.

This process continues in the second movement, which we might see as running from 1890 to about 1900. Here Yeats tries to express himself through a symbolic system which drew its images both from the individual mind in touch with a greater collective unconscious (the *Anima Mundi*) through the communal sources of myth and folklore, and from a learned but hidden tradition, the tradition of Cabbalistic studies, of Rosicrucian rituals, of Hermetic mysteries and esoteric gnosticism. Through Symbolism Yeats hoped to find a more exact expression than he had hitherto achieved, and to write poetry that would negotiate a shared ground between the individual imagination, the transcendental world of ideas, and the social world of everyday life. This symbolic endeavour is felt clearly in that section of the *Collected Poems* called *The Rose*, a name he adopted because here he felt that he had found 'the only pathway whereon he can hope to see with his own eyes the Eternal Rose of Beauty and of Peace'. The image also takes on a personal intensity through its association with Maud Gonne, the statuesque beauty and political activist he had met in January

1889, and whom he loved unavailingly for at least the next quarter of a century. *The Rose* is made up for the most part of poems that appeared in *The Countess Kathleen and Various Legends and Lyrics*, published in September 1892, but his next book of verse, *The Wind Among the Reeds*, although first announced in 1893 did not appear until 1899. The delay was caused by a number of factors. Now living in London, Yeats had helped found an informal society of poets, the Rhymers' Club, and they, and particularly his friend Lionel Johnson, made him intensely self-conscious about the form and technique of his work: each poem had to be perfect of its kind, and this took endless writing and rewritings. Another problem was, perhaps, even more intractable: he was unsure of his way. He was a man pulled in different directions. An apparently wholehearted belief in the transcendental value of the symbol was undercut by a lurking scepticism; sexual desire was frustrated by Maud Gonne's unwillingness to marry him or consummate their relationship; at times he felt himself to have a leading part in what he described to John O'Leary as the spiritual renaissance now abroad in the world, but somehow the tocsin of this great new awakening failed to sound clearly: he was left with ambiguous muffled sounds and he oscillated between confidence and foreboding. He was adrift, as he later described it, on the Hodos Chameliontos, the Path of the Chameleon, where 'image called up image in an endless procession, and I could not always choose among them with any confidence'.

'Then in 1900', Yeats later recalled, 'everybody got down off his stilts'. *The Wind Among the Reeds* is his most symbolist book of poems, a sustained brooding upon the dangerous forces of passion and the mysterious workings of consciousness and the subconscious, and, part of a fin-de-siècle zeitgeist, it was published, significantly, within a few months of Freud's *The Interpretation of Dreams*. Yet Yeats went no further in this style. There is an abrupt change of theme and idiom between 1899 and the poems which appeared in *In the Seven Woods* only five years later. *In the Seven Woods* (1904) inaugurates what we might describe as the third movement in Yeats's career, a phase that lasts until *Responsibilities* of 1914, and the first poem in the earlier book, 'In the Seven Woods', is matched by the final poem of *Responsibilities*. Both praise Coole Park, the Galway estate of his friend and patron Lady Gregory, as a necessary refuge from the meretriciousness and maliciousness of the contemporary world. In the nineties Yeats was intrigued by the Imagination's potential for mystical revelation, and for creating cultural cohesion. Now, aware of the fractiousness of modern society, and less sure of the power of symbols, he finds himself obliged to 'wither into the truth'.

The reasons for this change are many and complex. The experience of producing his plays after the foundation of the Irish Literary Theatre (later the Abbey Theatre) in 1899 led him to reflect upon his style. He found that his earlier manner was too picturesque, and he began to develop a poetry that relied for its effect upon verb rather than adjective and that gained its power from its syntactical and rhythmical energy rather than its descriptive felicities. This style became a fitting vehicle for his new themes, for, besides revising his attitude to poetic technique, the production of his plays also taught him that his ideas on art and life were repugnant to a significant and increasingly vocal section of that Irish audience in whom he had invested his hopes of a cultural revival. His plays were attacked, both in the press and in the theatre itself, as were those of his friend John Synge. He detected the growth of a philistine middle class in Ireland which had deceived itself into accepting the inferior artistic canons of taste prevalent in other nations, and this belief, registered in poems such as 'September 1913', was intensified by Dublin's refusal to build a gallery to house a collection of pictures donated to the city by his friend Hugh Lane.

These public disputes were mirrored by personal turmoil. He was devastated when Maud Gonne married another man, John MacBride, in 1903, but the relationship continued to haunt him, as she turned to him for advice when the marriage began to go wrong. A glorious row in the Golden Dawn called into question the origins of that magical society, and to an extent undermined his faith in the power of symbolism. Henceforth his symbols take their energy from their context in individual poems, rather than from supposed pre-ordained associations. His reading of the German philosopher Nietzsche developed his notion of the mask, and led him to celebrate what he was to call 'tragic joy', the ability to accept defeat and tragedy with fortitude and gaiety. At the same time his study of Castiglione's *The Book of the Courtier* confirmed his views on the necessity for an aristocratic code of courtesy and ceremony and the cultivation of that imaginative nonchalance called in Italian *sprezzatura*.

He summed up the lessons of these years and the effect on his work in a letter of 1913: 'Of recent years instead of "vision" meaning by vision the intense realization of a state of ecstatic emotions symbolized in a definite imagined pattern, I have tried for more self-portraiture, I have tried to make my work convincing with a speech so natural and dramatic that the hearer would feel the presence of a man thinking and feeling.' Most of the rest of his verse grows out of this ambition, but he was to find it necessary to explore the gap between self and self-portraiture more fully, and to expend much effort on shaping a speech that would seem natural and dramatic.

It was now that History began to overtake him. The idealism and self-sacrifice displayed by the Dublin insurrectionaries in the Easter Rising of 1916 revealed that he had been over-hasty in bidding farewell to 'Romantic Ireland' in 1913, but the bloodiness of the First World War, followed by the atrocities of the Anglo-Irish War and the Irish Civil War, forced him to review his position as a poet and as an ageing man. The great meditative poems of *The Tower* reflect upon the nature of poetic responsibility, ponder the relationship of the body to the soul, question the ability of the imagination to defy physical decrepitude and death, and brood upon the significance of an individual life to the larger sweep of history.

These meditations continue in his later poems, but here the cyclical historical system he worked out his book *A Vision* provides him with a mechanism – in poems such as 'The Gyres' and 'Lapis Lazuli' – for apprehending and confronting the otherwise inevitable (as he saw it) degeneration of the modern age. In politics he became more authoritarian, and was even briefly involved with the Irish Blue Shirt Movement, a movement which, while stemming from a peculiarly Irish situation and not to be easily equated with European Fascism, nevertheless had anti-democratic implications. Paradoxically, as his political stance grew more autocratic, his poetry became more anarchic and suspicious of establishments, celebrating those dissidents on the outspoken margins like Crazy Jane, and he himself adopted the guise of 'The Wild Wicked Old Man'.

Above all he refused to go gently into the good night of death. His last poems are shot through with defiant energy, and, when his poetic inspiration falters, he even writes a passionate poem, 'The Circus Animals Desertion', on the very lack of theme. In a letter written a few days before his death Yeats said that 'Man can embody truth but he cannot know it'. His collected poems are the embodiment of his attempt to bear truthful witness to his own life and to his voyage through the turbulence of the Modernist period. In the honesty of that witness they have become, as Eliot perceived, part of the consciousness of that age.

JOHN KELLY

A Note on The Text

The text and ordering of Yeats's poems has been the subject of much debate. This edition follows in the main the text and sequence of the Variorum Edition, except that the later poems are arranged in what is taken to be Yeats's final wishes, except that the epitaph from 'Under Ben Bulben' is published last.

W. B. Yeats

The Stolen Child

Where dips the rocky highland
Of Sleuth Wood in the lake,
There lies a leafy island
Where flapping herons wake
The drowsy water-rats;   5
There we've hid our faery vats,
Full of berries
And of reddest stolen cherries.
Come away, O human child!
To the waters and the wild   10
With a faery, hand in hand,
For the world's more full of weeping than you can understand.

Where the wave of moonlight glosses
The dim grey sands with light,
Far off by furthest Rosses   15
We foot it all the night,
Weaving olden dances,
Mingling hands and mingling glances
Till the moon has taken flight;
To and fro we leap   20
And chase the frothy bubbles,
While the world is full of troubles
And is anxious in its sleep.
Come away, O human child!
To the waters and the wild   25
With a faery, hand in hand,
For the world's more full of weeping than you can understand.

Where the wandering water gushes
From the hills above Glen-Car,
In pools among the rushes   30
That scarce could bathe a star,
We seek for slumbering trout
And whispering in their ears

Give them unquiet dreams;
Leaning softly out   35
From ferns that drop their tears
Over the young streams.
Come away, O human child!
To the waters and the wild
With a faery, hand in hand,   40
For the world's more full of weeping than you can understand.

Away with us he's going,
The solemn-eyed:
He'll hear no more the lowing
Of the calves on the warm hillside   45
Or the kettle on the hob
Sing peace into his breast,
Or see the brown mice bob
Round and round the oatmeal-chest.
For he comes, the human child,   50
To the waters and the wild
With a faery, hand in hand,
From a world more full of weeping than he can understand.

Down by the Salley Gardens

Down by the salley gardens my love and I did meet;
She passed the salley gardens with little snow-white feet.
She bid me take love easy, as the leaves grow on the tree;
But I, being young and foolish, with her would not agree.

In a field by the river my love and I did stand,   5
And on my leaning shoulder she laid her snow-white hand.
She bid me take life easy, as the grass grows on the weirs;
But I was young and foolish, and now am full of tears.

To the Rose upon the Rood of Time

Red Rose, proud Rose, sad Rose of all my days!
Come near me, while I sing the ancient ways:
Cuchulain battling with the bitter tide;
The Druid, grey, wood-nurtured, quiet-eyed,
Who cast round Fergus dreams, and ruin untold: 5
And thine own sadness, whereof stars, grown old
In dancing silver-sandalled on the sea,
Sing in their high and lonely melody.
Come near, that no more blinded by man's fate,
I find under the boughs of love and hate,   10
In all poor foolish things that live a day,
Eternal beauty wandering on her way.

Come near, come near, come near – Ah, leave me still
A little space for the rose-breath to fill!
Lest I no more hear common things that crave;   15
The weak worm hiding down in its small cave,
The field-mouse running by me in the grass,
And heavy mortal hopes that toil and pass,
But seek alone to hear the strange things said
By God to the bright hearts of those long dead,   20
And learn to chaunt a tongue men do not know.
Come near; I would, before my time to go,
Sing of old Eire and the ancient ways:
Red Rose, proud Rose, sad Rose of all my days.

The Lake Isle of Innisfree

I will arise and go now, and go to Innisfree,
And a small cabin build there, of clay and wattles made:
Nine bean-rows will I have there, a hive for the honey-bee,
And live alone in the bee-loud glade.

And I shall have some peace there, for peace comes dropping slow,   5
Dropping from the veils of the morning to where the cricket sings;
There midnight's all a glimmer, and noon a purple glow,
And evening full of the linnet's wings.

I will arise and go now, for always night and day
I hear lake water lapping with low sounds by the shore;   10
While I stand on the roadway, or on the pavements grey,
I hear it in the deep heart's core.

The Sorrow of Love

The brawling of a sparrow in the eaves,
The brilliant moon and all the milky sky,
And all that famous harmony of leaves,
Had blotted out man's image and his cry.

A girl arose that had red mournful lips   5
And seemed the greatness of the world in tears,
Doomed like Odysseus and the labouring ships
And proud as Priam murdered with his peers;

Arose, and on the instant clamorous eaves,
A climbing moon upon an empty sky,   10
And all that lamentation of the leaves,
Could but compose man's image and his cry.

When You are Old

When you are old and grey and full of sleep,
And nodding by the fire, take down this book,
And slowly read, and dream of the soft look
Your eyes had once, and of their shadows deep;

How many loved your moments of glad grace,   5
And loved your beauty with love false or true,
But one man loved the pilgrim soul in you,
And loved the sorrows of your changing face;

And bending down beside the glowing bars,
Murmur, a little sadly, how Love fled   10
And paced upon the mountains overhead
And hid his face amid a crowd of stars.

Who Goes with Fergus?

Who will go drive with Fergus now,
And pierce the deep wood's woven shade,
And dance upon the level shore?
Young man, lift up your russet brow,
And lift your tender eyelids, maid,   5
And brood on hopes and fear no more.

And no more turn aside and brood
Upon love's bitter mystery;
For Fergus rules the brazen cars,
And rules the shadows of the wood,   10
And the white breast of the dim sea
And all dishevelled wandering stars.

The Man who Dreamed of Faeryland

He stood among a crowd at Drumahair;
His heart hung all upon a silken dress,
And he had known at last some tenderness,
Before earth took him to her stony care;
But when a man poured fish into a pile,   5
It seemed they raised their little silver heads,
And sang what gold morning or evening sheds
Upon a woven world-forgotten isle
Where people love beside the ravelled seas;
That Time can never mar a lover's vows   10
Under that woven changeless roof of boughs:
The singing shook him out of his new ease.

He wandered by the sands of Lissadell;
His mind ran all on money cares and fears,
And he had known at last some prudent years   15
Before they heaped his grave under the hill;
But while he passed before a plashy place,
A lug-worm with its grey and muddy mouth
Sang that somewhere to north or west or south
There dwelt a gay, exulting, gentle race   20
Under the golden or the silver skies;
That if a dancer stayed his hungry foot
It seemed the sun and moon were in the fruit:
And at that singing he was no more wise.

He mused beside the well of Scanavin,   25
He mused upon his mockers: without fail
His sudden vengeance were a country tale,
When earthy night had drunk his body in;
But one small knot-grass growing by the pool
Sang where – unnecessary cruel voice –   30
Old silence bids its chosen race rejoice,
Whatever ravelled waters rise and fall
Or stormy silver fret the gold of day,
And midnight there enfold them like a fleece

And lover there by lover be at peace.   35
The tale drove his fine angry mood away.

He slept under the hill of Lugnagall;
And might have known at last unhaunted sleep
Under that cold and vapour-turbaned steep,
Now that the earth had taken man and all: 40
Did not the worms that spired about his bones
Proclaim with that unwearied, reedy cry
That God has laid His fingers on the sky,
That from those fingers glittering summer runs
Upon the dancer by the dreamless wave.   45
Why should those lovers that no lovers miss
Dream, until God burn Nature with a kiss?
The man has found no comfort in the grave.

To Ireland in the Coming Times

Know, that I would accounted be
True brother of a company
That sang, to sweeten Ireland's wrong,
Ballad and story, rann and song;
Nor be I any less of them,   5
Because the red-rose-bordered hem
Of her, whose history began
Before God made the angelic clan,
Trails all about the written page.   10
When Time began to rant and rage
The measure of her flying feet
Made Ireland's heart begin to beat;
And Time bade all his candles flare
To light a measure here and there;
And may the thoughts of Ireland brood   15
Upon a measured quietude.

Nor may I less be counted one
With Davis, Mangan, Ferguson,

Because, to him who ponders well,
My rhymes more than their rhyming tell   20
Of things discovered in the deep,
Where only body's laid asleep.
For the elemental creatures go
About my table to and fro,
That hurry from unmeasured mind   25
To rant and rage in flood and wind;
Yet he who treads in measured ways
May surely barter gaze for gaze.
Man ever journeys on with them
After the red-rose-bordered hem.   30
Ah, faeries, dancing under the moon,
A Druid land, a Druid tune!

While still I may, I write for you
The love I lived, the dream I knew.
From our birthday, until we die,   35
Is but the winking of an eye;
And we, our singing and our love,
What measurer Time has lit above,
And all benighted things that go
About my table to and fro,   40
Are passing on to where may be,
In truth's consuming ecstasy,
No place for love and dream at all;
For God goes by with white footfall.
I cast my heart into my rhymes,   45
That you, in the dim coming times,
May know how my heart went with them
After the red-rose-bordered hem.

The Hosting of the Sidhe

The host is riding from Knocknarea
And over the grave of Clooth-na-Bare;
Caoilte tossing his burning hair,
And Niamh calling *Away, come away:*
Empty your heart of its mortal dream.
The winds awaken, the leaves whirl round,   5
Our cheeks are pale, our hair is unbound,
Our breasts are heaving, our eyes are agleam,
Our arms are waving, our lips are apart;
And if any gaze on our rushing band,   10
We come between him and the deed of his hand,
We come between him and the hope of his heart.
The host is rushing 'twixt night and day,
And where is there hope or deed as fair?
Caoilte tossing his burning hair,   15
And Niamh calling *Away, come away.*

The Lover tells of the Rose in his Heart

All things uncomely and broken, all things worn out and old,
The cry of a child by the roadway, the creak of a lumbering
   cart,
The heavy steps of the ploughman, splashing the wintry
   mould,
Are wronging your image that blossoms a rose in the deeps of
   my heart.

The wrong of unshapely things is a wrong too great to be
   told;   5
I hunger to build them anew and sit on a green knoll apart,
With the earth and the sky and the water, re-made, like a
   casket of gold
For my dreams of your image that blossoms a rose in the deeps
   of my heart.

The Song of Wandering Aengus

I went out to the hazel wood,
Because a fire was in my head,
And cut and peeled a hazel wand,
And hooked a berry to a thread;
And when white moths were on the wing,   5
And moth-like stars were flickering out,
I dropped the berry in a stream
And caught a little silver trout.

When I had laid it on the floor
I went to blow the fire aflame,   10
But something rustled on the floor,
And some one called me by my name:
It had become a glimmering girl
With apple blossom in her hair
Who called me by my name and ran   15
And faded through the brightening air.

Though I am old with wandering
Through hollow lands and hilly lands,
I will find out where she has gone,
And kiss her lips and take her hands;   20
And walk among long dappled grass,
And pluck till time and times are done
The silver apples of the moon,
The golden apples of the sun.

He bids his Beloved be at Peace

I hear the Shadowy Horses, their long manes a-shake,
Their hoofs heavy with tumult, their eyes glimmering white;
The North unfolds above them clinging, creeping night,
The East her hidden joy before the morning break,
The West weeps in pale dew and sighs passing away,   5
The South is pouring down roses of crimson fire:
O vanity of Sleep, Hope, Dream, endless Desire,
The Horses of Disaster plunge in the heavy clay:
Beloved, let your eyes half close, and your heart beat
Over my heart, and your hair fall over my breast,   10
Drowning love's lonely hour in deep twilight of rest,
And hiding their tossing manes and their tumultuous feet.

He remembers Forgotten Beauty

When my arms wrap you round I press
My heart upon the loveliness
That has long faded from the world;
The jewelled crowns that kings have hurled
In shadowy pools, when armies fled;   5
The love-tales wrought with silken thread
By dreaming ladies upon cloth
That has made fat the murderous moth;
The roses that of old time were
Woven by ladies in their hair,   10
The dew-cold lilies ladies bore
Through many a sacred corridor
Where such grey clouds of incense rose
That only God's eyes did not close:
For that pale breast and lingering hand   15
Come from a more dream-heavy land,
A more dream-heavy hour than this;

And when you sigh from kiss to kiss
I hear white Beauty sighing, too,
For hours when all must fade like dew,   20
But flame on flame, and deep on deep,
Throne on throne where in half sleep,
Their swords upon their iron knees,
Brood her high lonely mysteries.

The Valley of the Black Pig

The dews drop slowly and dreams gather: unknown spears
Suddenly hurtle before my dream-awakened eyes,
And then the clash of fallen horsemen and the cries
Of unknown perishing armies beat about my ears.
We who still labour by the cromlech on the shore,   5
The grey cairn on the hill, when day sinks drowned in dew,
Being weary of the world's empires, bow down to you,
Master of the still stars and of the flaming door.

The Secret Rose

Far-off, most secret, and inviolate Rose,
Enfold me in my hour of hours; where those
Who sought thee in the Holy Sepulchre,
Or in the wine-vat, dwell beyond the stir
And tumult of defeated dreams; and deep   5
Among pale eyelids, heavy with the sleep
Men have named beauty. Thy great leaves enfold
The ancient beards, the helms of ruby and gold
Of the crowned Magi; and the king whose eyes
Saw the Pierced Hands and Rood of elder rise   10
In Druid vapour and make the torches dim;

Till vain frenzy awoke and he died; and him
Who met Fand walking among flaming dew
By a grey shore where the wind never blew,
And lost the world and Emer for a kiss;   15
And him who drove the gods out of their liss,
And till a hundred morns had flowered red
Feasted, and wept the barrows of his dead;
And the proud dreaming king who flung the crown   20
And sorrow away, and calling bard and clown
Dwelt among wine-stained wanderers in deep woods;
And him who sold tillage, and house, and goods,
And sought through lands and islands numberless years,
Until he found, with laughter and with tears,
A woman of so shining loveliness   25
That men threshed corn at midnight by a tress,
A little stolen tress. I, too, await
The hour of thy great wind of love and hate.
When shall the stars be blown about the sky,
Like the sparks blown out of a smithy, and die?   30
Surely thine hour has come, thy great wind blows,
Far-off, most secret, and inviolate Rose?

He wishes for the Cloths of Heaven

Had I the heavens' embroidered cloths,
Enwrought with golden and silver light,
The blue and the dim and the dark cloths
Of night and light and the half-light,
I would spread the cloths under your feet: 5
But I, being poor, have only my dreams;
I have spread my dreams under your feet;
Tread softly because you tread on my dreams.

The Fiddler of Dooney

When I play on my fiddle in Dooney,
Folk dance like a wave of the sea;
My cousin is priest in Kilvarnet,
My brother in Mocharabuiee.

I passed my brother and cousin: 5
They read in their books of prayer;
I read in my book of songs
I bought at the Sligo fair.

When we come at the end of time
To Peter sitting in state,   10
He will smile on the three old spirits,
But call me first through the gate;

For the good are always the merry,
Save by an evil chance,
And the merry love the fiddle,   15
And the merry love to dance:

And when the folk there spy me,
They will all come up to me,
With 'Here is the fiddler of Dooney!'
And dance like a wave of the sea.   20

In the Seven Woods

I have heard the pigeons of the Seven Woods
Make their faint thunder, and the garden bees
Hum in the lime-tree flowers; and put away
The unavailing outcries and the old bitterness
That empty the heart. I have forgot awhile   5
Tara uprooted, and new commonness

Upon the throne and crying about the streets
And hanging its paper flowers from post to post,
Because it is alone of all things happy.
I am contented, for I know that Quiet   10
Wanders laughing and eating her wild heart
Among pigeons and bees, while that Great Archer,
Who but awaits His hour to shoot, still hangs
A cloudy quiver over Pairc-na-lee.

The Folly of Being Comforted

One that is ever kind said yesterday:
'Your well-beloved's hair has threads of grey,
And little shadows come about her eyes;
Time can but make it easier to be wise
Though now it seems impossible, and so   5
All that you need is patience.'
                                        Heart cries, 'No,
I have not a crumb of comfort, not a grain.
Time can but make her beauty over again:
Because of that great nobleness of hers
The fire that stirs about her, when she stirs,   10
Burns but more clearly. O she had not these ways
When all the wild summer was in her gaze.'

O heart! O heart! if she'd but turn her head,
You'd know the folly of being comforted.

Never Give all the Heart

Never give all the heart, for love
Will hardly seem worth thinking of
To passionate women if it seem
Certain, and they never dream
That it fades out from kiss to kiss;   5
For everything that's lovely is
But a brief, dreamy, kind delight.
O never give the heart outright,
For they, for all smooth lips can say,
Have given their hearts up to the play.   10
And who could play it well enough
If deaf and dumb and blind with love?
He that made this knows all the cost,
For he gave all his heart and lost.

Adam's Curse

We sat together at one summer's end,
That beautiful mild woman, your close friend,
And you and I, and talked of poetry.
I said: 'A line will take us hours maybe;
Yet if it does not seem a moment's thought,   5
Our stitching and unstitching has been naught.
Better go down upon your marrow-bones
And scrub a kitchen pavement, or break stones
Like an old pauper, in all kinds of weather;
For to articulate sweet sounds together   10
Is to work harder than all these, and yet
Be thought an idler by the noisy set
Of bankers, schoolmasters, and clergymen
The martyrs call the world.'

                                        And thereupon

That beautiful mild woman for whose sake 15
There's many a one shall find out all heartache
On finding that her voice is sweet and low
Replied: 'To be born woman is to know –
Although they do not talk of it at school –
That we must labour to be beautiful.' 20
I said: 'It's certain there is no fine thing
Since Adam's fall but needs much labouring.
There have been lovers who thought love should be
So much compounded of high courtesy
That they would sigh and quote with learned looks 25
Precedents out of beautiful old books;
Yet now it seems an idle trade enough.'

We sat grown quiet at the name of love;
We saw the last embers of daylight die,
And in the trembling blue-green of the sky
A moon, worn as if it had been a shell 30
Washed by time's waters as they rose and fell
About the stars and broke in days and years.

I had a thought for no one's but your ears:
That you were beautiful, and that I strove 35
To love you in the old high way of love;
That it had all seemed happy, and yet we'd grown
As weary-hearted as that hollow moon.

Words

I had this thought a while ago,
'My darling cannot understand
What I have done, or what would do
In this blind bitter land.'

And I grew weary of the sun 5
Until my thoughts cleared up again,

Remembering that the best I have done
Was done to make it plain;

That every year I have cried, 'At length
My darling understands it all,   10
Because I have come into my strength,
And words obey my call';

That had she done so who can say
What would have shaken from the sieve?
I might have thrown poor words away   15
And been content to live.

No Second Troy

Why should I blame her that she filled my days
With misery, or that she would of late
Have taught to ignorant men most violent ways,
Or hurled the little streets upon the great,
Had they but courage equal to desire?   5
What could have made her peaceful with a mind
That nobleness made simple as a fire,
With beauty like a tightened bow, a kind
That is not natural in an age like this,
Being high and solitary and most stern?   10
Why, what could she have done, being what she is?
Was there another Troy for her to burn?

All Things can Tempt me

All things can tempt me from this craft of verse:
One time it was a woman's face, or worse –
The seeming needs of my fool-driven land;
Now nothing but comes readier to the hand
Than this accustomed toil. When I was young,   5
I had not given a penny for a song
Did not the poet sing it with such airs
That one believed he had a sword upstairs;
Yet would be now, could I but have my wish,
Colder and dumber and deafer than a fish.   10

Pardon, old fathers, if you still remain
Somewhere in ear-shot for the story's end,
Old Dublin merchant 'free of the ten and four'
Or trading out of Galway into Spain;
Old country scholar, Robert Emmet's friend,   5
A hundred-year-old memory to the poor;
Merchant and scholar who have left me blood
That has not passed through any huckster's loin,
Soldiers that gave, whatever die was cast:
A Butler or an Armstrong that withstood   10
Beside the brackish waters of the Boyne
James and his Irish when the Dutchman crossed;
Old merchant skipper that leaped overboard
After a ragged hat in Bascay Bay;
You most of all, silent and fierce old man,   15
Because the daily spectacle that stirred
My fancy, and set my boyish lips to say,
'Only the wasteful virtues earn the sun';
Pardon that for a barren passion's sake,
Although I have come come close on forty-nine,   20
I have no child, I have nothing but a book,
Nothing but that to prove your blood and mine.

To a Wealthy Man who promised a Second Subscription to the Dublin Municipal Gallery if it were proved the People wanted Pictures

You gave, but will not give again
Until enough of Paudeen's pence
By Biddy's halfpennies have lain
To be 'some sort of evidence',
Before you'll put your guineas down,   5
That things it were a pride to give
Are what the blind and ignorant town
Imagines best to make it thrive.
What cared Duke Ercole, that bid
His mummers to the market-place,   10
What th'onion-sellers thought or did
So that his Plautus set the pace
For the Italian comedies?
And Guidobaldo, when he made
That grammar school of courtesies   15
Where wit and beauty learned their trade
Upon Urbino's windy hill,
Had sent no runners to and fro
That he might learn the shepherds' will.
And when they drove out Cosimo,   20
Indifferent how the rancour ran,
He gave the hours they had set free
To Michelozzo's latest plan
For the San Marco Library,
Whence turbulent Italy should draw   25
Delight in Art whose end is peace,
In logic and in natural law
By sucking at the dugs of Greece.

Your open hand but shows our loss,
For he knew better how to live.   30
Let Paudeens play at pitch and toss,

Look up in the sun's eye and give
What the exultant heart calls good
That some new day may breed the best
Because you gave, not what they would,   35
But the right twigs for an eagle's nest!

September 1913

What need you, being come to sense,
But fumble in a greasy till
And add the halfpence to the pence
And prayer to shivering prayer, until
You have dried the marrow from the bone?   5
For men were born to pray and save:
Romantic Ireland's dead and gone,
It's with O'Leary in the grave.

Yet they were of a different kind,
The names that stilled your childish play,   10
They have gone about the world like wind,
But little time had they to pray
For whom the hangman's rope was spun,
And what, God help us, could they save?
Romantic Ireland's dead and gone,   15
It's with O'Leary in the grave.

Was it for this the wild geese spread
The grey wing upon every tide;
For this that all that blood was shed,
For this Edward Fitzgerald died,   20
And Robert Emmet and Wolfe Tone,
All that delirium of the brave?
Romantic Ireland's dead and gone,
It's with O'Leary in the grave.

Yet could we turn the years again,   25
And call those exiles as they were

In all their loneliness and pain,
You'd cry, 'Some woman's yellow hair
Has maddened every mother's son':
They weighed so lightly what they gave.   30
But let them be, they're dead and gone,
They're with O'Leary in the grave.

Paudeen

Indignant at the fumbling wits, the obscure spite
Of our old Paudeen in his shop, I stumbled blind
Among the stones and thorn-trees, under morning light;
Until a curlew cried and in the luminous wind
A curlew answered; and suddenly thereupon I thought   5
That on the lonely height where all are in God's eye,
There cannot be, confusion of our sound forgot,
A single soul that lacks a sweet crystalline cry.

Friends

Now must I these three praise –
Three women that have wrought
What joy is in my days:
One because no thought,
Nor those unpassing cares,   5
No, not in these fifteen
Many-times-troubled years,
Could ever come between
Mind and delighted mind;
And one because her hand   10
Had strength that could unbind

What none can understand,
What none can have and thrive,
Youth's dreamy load, till she
So changed me that I live   15
Labouring in ecstasy.
And what of her that took
All till my youth was gone
With scarce a pitying look?
How could I praise that one?   20
When day begins to break
I count my good and bad,
Being wakeful for her sake,
Remembering what she had,
What eagle look still shows,   25
While up from my heart's root
So great a sweetness flows
I shake from head to foot.

The Cold Heaven

Suddenly I saw the cold and rook-delighting heaven
That seemed as though ice burned and was but the more ice,
And thereupon imagination and heart were driven
So wild that every casual thought of that and this
Vanished, and left but memories, that should be out of season   5
With the hot blood of youth, of love crossed long ago;
And I took all the blame out of all sense and reason,
Until I cried and trembled and rocked to and fro,
Riddled with light. Ah! when the ghost begins to quicken,
Confusion of the death-bed over, is it sent   10
Out naked on the roads, as the books say, and stricken
By the injustice of the skies for punishment?

The Magi

Now as at all times I can see in the mind's eye,
In their stiff, painted clothes, the pale unsatisfied ones
Appear and disappear in the blue depth of the sky
With all their ancient faces like rain-beaten stones,
And all their helms of silver hovering side by side,   5
And all their eyes still fixed, hoping to find once more,
Being by Calvary's turbulence unsatisfied,
The uncontrollable mystery on the bestial floor.

A Coat

I made my song a coat
Covered with embroideries
Out of old mythologies
From heel to throat;
But the fools caught it,   5
Wore it in the world's eyes
As though they'd wrought it.
Song, let them take it,
For there's more enterprise
In walking naked.   10

While I, from that reed-throated whisperer
Who comes at need, although not now as once
A clear articulation in the air,
But inwardly, surmise companions
Beyond the fling of the dull ass's hoof   5
— Ben Jonson's phrase — and find when June is come
At Kyle-na-no under that ancient roof
A sterner conscience and a friendlier home,

I can forgive even that wrong of wrongs,
Those undreamt accidents that have made me   10
– Seeing that Fame has perished this long while,
Being but a part of ancient ceremony –
Notorious, till all my priceless things
Are but a post the passing dogs defile.

The Wild Swans at Coole

The trees are in their autumn beauty,
The woodland paths are dry,
Under the October twilight the water
Mirrors a still sky;
Upon the brimming water among the stones   5
Are nine-and-fifty swans.

The nineteenth autumn has come upon me
Since I first made my count;
I saw, before I had well finished,
All suddenly mount   10
And scatter wheeling in great broken rings
Upon their clamorous wings.

I have looked upon those brilliant creatures,
And now my heart is sore.
All's changed since I, hearing at twilight,   15
The first time on this shore,
The bell-beat of their wings above my head,
Trod with a lighter tread.

Unwearied still, lover by lover,
They paddle in the cold   20
Companionable streams or climb the air;
Their hearts have not grown old;
Passion or conquest, wander where they will,
Attend upon them still.

But now they drift on the still water,   25
Mysterious, beautiful;
Among what rushes will they build,
By what lake's edge or pool
Delight men's eyes when I awake some day
To find they have flown away?   30

In Memory of Major Robert Gregory

I

Now that we're almost settled in our house
I'll name the friends that cannot sup with us
Beside a fire of turf in th'ancient tower,
And having talked to some late hour
Climb up the narrow winding stair to bed: 5
Discoverers of forgotten truth
Or mere companions of my youth,
All, all are in my thoughts to-night being dead.

II

Always we'd have the new friend meet the old
And we are hurt if either friend seem cold,
And there is salt to lengthen out the smart
In the affections of our heart,
And quarrels are blown up upon that head;   5
But not a friend that I would bring
This night can set us quarrelling,
For all that come into my mind are dead.

III

Lionel Johnson comes the first to mind,
That loved his learning better than mankind,
Though courteous to the worst; much falling he

Brooded upon sanctity
Till all his Greek and Latin learning seemed   5
A long blast upon the horn that brought
A little nearer to his thought
A measureless consummation that he dreamed.

IV

And that enquiring man John Synge comes next,
That dying chose the living world for text
And never could have rested in the tomb
But that, long travelling, he had come
Towards nightfall upon certain set apart   5
In a most desolate stony place,
Towards nightfall upon a race
Passionate and simple like his heart.

V

And then I think of old George Pollexfen,
In muscular youth well known to Mayo men
For horsemanship at meets or at racecourses,
That could have shown how pure-bred horses
And solid men, for all their passion, live   5
But as the outrageous stars incline
By opposition, square and trine;
Having grown sluggish and contemplative.

VI

They were my close companions many a year,
A portion of my mind and life, as it were,
And now their breathless faces seem to look
Out of some old picture-book;
I am accustomed to their lack of breath,   5
But not that my dear friend's dear son,
Our Sidney and our perfect man,
Could share in that discourtesy of death.

VII

For all things the delighted eye now sees
Were loved by him: the old storm broken trees
That cast their shadows upon road and bridge;
The tower set on the stream's edge;
The ford where drinking cattle make a stir   5
Nightly, and startled by that sound
The water-hen must changer her ground;
He might have been your heartiest welcomer.

VIII

When with the Galway foxhounds he would ride
From Castle Taylor to the Roxborough side
Or Esserkelly plain, few kept his pace;
At Mooneen he had leaped a place
So perilous that half the astonished meet   5
Had shut their eyes; and where was it
He rode a race without a bit?
And yet his mind outran the horses' feet.

IX

We dreamed that a great painter had been born
To cold Clare rock and Galway rock and thorn,
To that stern colour and that delicate line
That are our secret discipline
Wherein the gazing heart doubles her might.   5
Soldier, scholar, horseman, he,
And yet he had the intensity
To have published all to be a world's delight.

X

What other could so well have counselled us
In all lovely intricacies of a house
As he that practised or that understood
All work in metal or in wood,
In moulded plaster or in carven stone?   5
Soldier, scholar, horseman, he,

And all he did done perfectly
As though he had but that one trade alone.

XI

Some burn damp faggots, others may consume
The entire combustible world in one small room
As though dried straw, and if we turn about
The bare chimney is gone black out
Because the work had finished in that flare.   5
Soldier, scholar, horseman, he,
As 'twere all life's epitome.
What made us dream that he could comb grey hair?

XII

I had thought, seeing how bitter is that wind
That shakes the shutter, to have brought to mind
All those that manhood tried, or childhood loved
Or boyish intellect approved,
With some appropriate commentary on each;   5
Until imagination brought
A fitter welcome; but a thought
Of that late death took all my heart for speech.

An Irish Airman Foresees his Death

I know that I shall meet my fate
Somewhere among the clouds above;
Those that I fight I do not hate,
Those that I guard I do not love;
My country is Kiltartan Cross,   5
My countrymen Kiltartan's poor,
No likely end could bring them loss
Or leave them happier than before.
Nor law, nor duty bade me fight,

Nor public men, nor cheering crowds,   10
A lonely impulse of delight
Drove to this tumult in the clouds;
I balanced all, brought all to mind,
The years to come seemed waste of breath,
A waste of breath the years behind   15
In balance with this life, this death.

Lines Written in Dejection

When have I last looked on
The round green eyes and the long wavering bodies
Of the dark leopards of the moon?
All the wild witches, those most noble ladies,
For all their broom-sticks and their tears,   5
Their angry tears, are gone.
The holy centaurs of the hills are vanished;
I have nothing but the embittered sun;
Banished heroic mother moon and vanished,
And now that I have come to fifty years   10
I must endure the timid sun.

The Fisherman

Although I can see him still,
The freckled man who goes
To a grey place on a hill
In grey Connemara clothes
At dawn to cast his flies,   5
It's long since I began
To call up to the eyes
This wise and simple man.

All day I'd looked in the face
What I had hoped 'twould be   10
To write for my own race
And the reality;
The living men that I hate,
The dead man that I loved,
The craven man in his seat,   15
The insolent unreproved,
And no knave brought to book
Who has won a drunken cheer,
The witty man and his joke
Aimed at the commonest ear,   20
The clever man who cries
The catch-cries of the clown,
The beating down of the wise
And great Art beaten down.

Maybe a twelvemonth since   25
Suddenly I began,
In scorn of this audience,
Imagining a man,
And his sun-freckled face,
And grey Connemara cloth,   30
Climbing up to a place
Where stone is dark under froth,
And the down-turn of his wrist
When the flies drop in the stream;
A man who does not exist,   35
A man who is but a dream;
And cried, 'Before I am old
I shall have written him one
Poem maybe as cold
And passionate as the dawn.'   40

Memory

One had a lovely face,
And two or three had charm,
But charm and face were in vain
Because the mountain grass
Cannot but keep the form   5
Where the mountain hare has lain.

A Deep-Sworn Vow

Others because you did not keep
That deep-sworn vow have been friends of mine;
Yet always when I look death in the face,
When I clamber to the heights of sleep,
Or when I grow excited with wine,
Suddenly I meet your face.   5

Michael Robartes and the Dancer

He. Opinion is not worth a rush;
In this altar-piece the knight,
Who grips his long spear so to push
That dragon through the fading light,
Loved the lady; and it's plain   5
The half-dead dragon was her thought,
That every morning rose again
And dug its claws and shrieked and fought.
Could the impossible come to pass
She would have time to turn her eyes,   10
Her lover thought, upon the glass
And on the instant would grow wise.

She. You mean they argued.

He.   Put it so;
But bear in mind your lover's wage
Is what your looking-glass can show,   15
And that he will turn green with rage
At all that is not pictured there.

She. May I not put myself to college?

He. Go pluck Athene by the hair;
For what mere book can grant a knowledge   20
With an impassioned gravity
Appropriate to that beating breast,
That vigorous thigh, that dreaming eye?
And may the Devil take the rest.

She. And must no beautiful woman be
Learned like a man?   25

He.   Paul Veronese
And all his sacred company
Imagined bodies all their days
By the lagoon you love so much,
For proud, soft, ceremonious proof   30
That all must come to sight and touch;
While Michael Angelo's Sistine roof,
His 'Morning' and his 'Night' disclose
How sinew that has been pulled tight,
Or it may be loosened in repose,   35
Can rule by supernatural right
Yet be but sinew.

She.   I have heard said
There is great danger in the body.

He. Did God in portioning wine and bread
Give man His thought or His mere body?   40

She. My wretched dragon is perplexed.

He. I have principles to prove me right.
It follows from this Latin text
That blest souls are not composite,
And that all beautiful women may   45
Live in uncomposite blessedness,
And lead us to the like – if they
Will banish every thought, unless
The lineaments that please their view
When the long looking-glass is full,   50
Even from the foot-sole think it too.

She. They say such different things at school.

Easter 1916

I have met them at close of day
Coming with vivid faces
From counter or desk among grey
Eighteenth-century houses.
I have passed with a nod of the head   5
Or polite meaningless words,
Or have lingered awhile and said
Polite meaningless words,
And thought before I had done
Of a mocking tale or a gibe   10
To please a companion
Around the fire at the club,
Being certain that they and I
But lived where motley is worn:
All changed, changed utterly: 15
A terrible beauty is born.

That woman's days were spent
In ignorant good-will,
Her nights in argument
Until her voice grew shrill.   20

What voice more sweet than hers
When, young and beautiful,
She rode to harriers?
This man had kept a school
And rode our wingèd horse;   25
This other his helper and friend
Was coming into his force;
He might have won fame in the end,
So sensitive his nature seemed,
So daring and sweet his thought.   30
This other man I had dreamed
A drunken, vainglorious lout.
He had done most bitter wrong
To some who are near my heart,
Yet I number him in the song;   35
He, too, has resigned his part
In the casual comedy;
He, too, has been changed in his turn,
Transformed utterly:
A terrible beauty is born.   40

Hearts with one purpose alone
Through summer and winter seem
Enchanted to a stone
To trouble the living stream.
The horse that comes from the road,   45
The rider, the birds that range
From cloud to tumbling cloud,
Minute by minute they change;
A shadow of cloud on the stream
Changes minute by minute;   50
A horse-hoof slides on the brim,
And a horse plashes within it;
The long-legged moor-hens dive,
And hens to moor-cocks call;
Minute by minute they live: 55
The stone's in the midst of all.

Too long a sacrifice
Can make a stone of the heart.

O when may it suffice?
That is Heaven's part, our part   60
To murmur name upon name,
As a mother names her child
When sleep at last has come
On limbs that had run wild.
What is it but nightfall?   65
No, no, not night but death;
Was it needless death after all?
For England may keep faith
For all that is done and said.
We know their dream; enough   70
To know they dreamed and are dead;
And what if excess of love
Bewildered them till they died?
I write it out in a verse –
MacDonagh and MacBride   75
And Connolly and Pearse
Now and in time to be,
Wherever green is worn,
Are changed, changed utterly:
A terrible beauty is born.   80

On a Political Prisoner

She that but little patience knew,
From childhood on, had now so much
A grey gull lost its fear and flew
Down to her cell and there alit,
And there endured her fingers' touch   5
And from her fingers ate its bit.

Did she in touching that lone wing
Recall the years before her mind
Because a bitter, an abstract thing,

Her thought some popular enmity: 10
Blind and leader of the blind
Drinking the foul ditch where they lie?

When long ago I saw her ride
Under Ben Bulben to the meet,
The beauty of her country-side   15
With all youth's lonely wildness stirred,
She seemed to have grown clean and sweet
Like any rock-bred, sea-borne bird:

Sea-borne, or balanced on the air
When first it sprang out of the nest   20
Upon some lofty rock to stare
Upon the cloudy canopy,
While under its storm-beaten breast
Cried out the hollows of the sea.

The Second Coming

Turning and turning in the widening gyre
The falcon cannot hear the falconer;
Things fall apart; the centre cannot hold;
Mere anarchy is loosed upon the world,
The blood-dimmed tide is loosed, and everywhere   5
The ceremony of innocence is drowned;
The best lack all conviction, while the worst
Are full of passionate intensity.

Surely some revelation is at hand;
Surely the Second Coming is at hand.   10
The Second Coming! Hardly are those words out
When a vast image out of *Spiritus Mundi*
Troubles my sight: somewhere in sands of the desert
A shape with lion body and the head of a man,
A gaze blank and pitiless as the sun,   15

Is moving its slow thighs, while all about it
Reel shadows of the indignant desert birds.
The darkness drops again; but now I know
That twenty centuries of stony sleep
Were vexed to nightmare by a rocking cradle,   20
And what rough beast, its hour come round at last,
Slouches towards Bethlehem to be born?

A Prayer for my Daughter

Once more the storm is howling, and half hid
Under this cradle-hood and coverlid
My child sleeps on. There is no obstacle
But Gregory's wood and one bare hill
Whereby the haystack- and roof-levelling wind,   5
Bred on the Atlantic, can be stayed;
And for an hour I have walked and prayed
Because of the great gloom that is in my mind.

I have walked and prayed for this young child an hour
And heard the sea-wind scream upon the tower,   10
And under the arches of the bridge, and scream
In the elms above the flooded stream;
Imagining in excited reverie
That the future years had come,
Dancing to a frenzied drum,   15
Out of the murderous innocence of the sea.

May she be granted beauty and yet not
Beauty to make a stranger's eye distraught,
Or hers before a looking-glass, for such,
Being made beautiful overmuch,   20
Consider beauty a sufficient end,
Lose natural kindness and maybe
The heart-revealing intimacy
That chooses right, and never find a friend.

Helen being chosen found life flat and dull 25
And later had much trouble from a fool,
While that great Queen, that rose out of the spray,
Being fatherless could have her way
Yet chose a bandy-leggèd smith for man.
It's certain that fine women eat 30
A crazy salad with their meat
Whereby the Horn of Plenty is undone.

In courtesy I'd have her chiefly learned;
Hearts are not had as a gift but hearts are earned
By those that are not entirely beautiful; 35
Yet many, that have played the fool
For beauty's very self, has charm made wise,
And many a poor man that has roved,
Loved and thought himself beloved,
From a glad kindness cannot take his eyes. 40

May she become a flourishing hidden tree
That all her thoughts may like the linnet be,
And have no business but dispensing round
Their magnanimities of sound,
Nor but in merriment begin a chase, 45
Nor but in merriment a quarrel.
O may she live like some green laurel
Rooted in one dear perpetual place.

My mind, because the minds that I have loved,
The sort of beauty that I have approved, 50
Prosper but little, has dried up of late,
Yet knows that to be choked with hate
May well be of all evil chances chief.
If there's no hatred in a mind
Assault and battery of the wind 55
Can never tear the linnet from the leaf.

An intellectual hatred is the worst,
So let her think opinions are accursed.
Have I not seen the loveliest woman born
Out of the mouth of Plenty's horn, 60

Because of her opinionated mind
Barter that horn and every good
By quiet natures understood
For an old bellows full of angry wind?

Considering that, all hatred driven hence,   65
The soul recovers radical innocence
And learns at last that it is self-delighting,
Self-appeasing, self-affrighting,
And that its own sweet will is Heaven's will;
She can, though ever face should scowl   70
And every windy quarter howl
Or every bellows burst, be happy still.

And may her bridegroom bring her to a house
Where all's accustomed, ceremonious;
For arrogance and hatred are the wares
Peddled in the thoroughfares.   75
How but in custom and in ceremony
Are innocence and beauty born?
Ceremony's a name for the rich horn,
And custom for the spreading laurel tree.   80

Sailing to Byzantium

I

That is no country for old men. The young
In one another's arms, birds in the trees
– Those dying generations – at their song,
The salmon-falls, the mackerel-crowded seas,
Fish, flesh, or fowl, commend all summer long   5
Whatever is begotten, born, and dies.
Caught in that sensual music all neglect
Monuments of unageing intellect.

II

An aged man is but a paltry thing,
A tattered coat upon a stick, unless
Soul clap its hands and sing, and louder sing
For every tatter in its mortal dress,
Nor is there singing school but studying 5
Monuments of its own magnificence;
And therefore I have sailed the seas and come
To the holy city of Byzantium.

III

O sages standing in God's holy fire
As in the gold mosaic of a wall,
Come from the holy fire, perne in a gyre,
And be the singing-masters of my soul.
Consume my heart away; sick with desire 5
And fastened to a dying animal
It knows not what it is; and gather me
Into the artifice of eternity.

IV

Once out of nature I shall never take
My bodily form from any natural thing,
But such a form as Grecian goldsmiths make
Of hammered gold and gold enamelling
To keep a drowsy Emperor awake; 5
Or set upon a golden bough to sing
To lords and ladies of Byzantium
Of what is past, or passing, or to come.

The Tower

I

What shall I do with this absurdity—
O heart, O troubled heart— this caricature,
Decrepit age that has been tied to me
As to a dog's tail?
                Never had I more
Excited, passionate, fantastical   5
Imagination, nor an ear and eye
That more expected the impossible—
No, not in boyhood when with rod and fly,
Or the humbler worm, I climbed Ben Bulben's back
And had the livelong summer day to spend.   10
It seems that I must bid the Muse go pack,
Choose Plato and Plotinus for a friend
Until imagination, ear and eye,
Can be content with argument and deal
In abstract things; or be derided by   15
A sort of battered kettle at the heel.

II

I pace upon the battlements and stare
On the foundations of a house, or where
Tree, like a sooty finger, starts from the earth;
And send imagination forth
Under the day's declining beam, and call   5
Images and memories
From ruin or from ancient trees,
For I would ask a question of them all.

Beyond that ridge lived Mrs French, and once
When every silver candlestick or sconce   10
Lit up the dark mahogany and the wine,
A serving-man, that could divine
That most respected lady's every wish,
Ran and with the garden shears

Clipped an insolent farmer's ears   15
And brought them in a little covered dish.

Some few remembered still when I was young
A peasant girl commended by a song,
Who'd lived somewhere upon that rocky place,
And praised the colour of her face,   20
And had the greater joy in praising her,
Remembering that, if walked she there,
Farmers jostled at the fair
So great a glory did the song confer.

And certain men, being maddened by those rhymes,   25
Or else by toasting her a score of times,
Rose from the table and declared it right
To test their fancy by their sight;
But they mistook the brightness of the moon
For the prosaic light of day—   30
Music had driven their wits astray —
And one was drowned in the great bog of Cloone.

Strange, but the man who made the song was blind;
Yet, now I have considered it, I find
That nothing strange; the tragedy began   35
With Homer that was a blind man,
And Helen has all living hearts betrayed.
O may the moon and sunlight seem
One inextricable beam,
For if I triumph I must make men mad.   40

And I myself created Hanrahan
And drove him drunk or sober through the dawn
From somewhere in the neighbouring cottages.
Caught by an old man's juggleries
He stumbled, tumbled, fumbled to and fro   45
And had but broken knees for hire
And horrible splendour of desire;
I thought it all out twenty years ago:

Good fellows shuffled cards in an old bawn;
And when that ancient ruffian's turn was on   50

He so bewitched the cards under his thumb
That all but the one card became
A pack of hounds and not a pack of cards,
And that he changed into a hare.
Hanrahan rose in frenzy there   55
And followed up those baying creatures towards –

O towards I have forgotten what – enough!
I must recall a man that neither love
Nor music nor an enemy's clipped ear
Could, he was so harried, cheer;   60
A figure that has grown so fabulous
There's not a neighbour left to say
When he finished his dog's day:
An ancient bankrupt master of this house.

Before that ruin came, for centuries,   65
Rough men-at-arms, cross-gartered to the knees
Or shod in iron, climbed the narrow stairs,
And certain men-at-arms there were
Whose images, in the Great Memory stored,
Come with loud cry and panting breast   70
To break upon a sleepers rest
While their great wooden dice beat on the board.

As I would question all, come all who can;
Come old, necessitous. half-mounted man;
And bring beauty's blind rambling celebrant;   75
The red man the juggler sent
Through God-forsaken meadows; Mrs. French,
Gifted with so fine an ear;
The man drowned in a bog's mire,
When mocking Muses chose the country wench.   80

Did all old men and women, rich and poor,
Who trod upon these rocks or passed this door,
Whether in public or in secret rage
As I do now against old age?
But I have found an answer in those eyes   85
That are impatient to be gone;

Go therefore; but leave Hanrahan,
For I need all his mighty memories.

Old lecher with a love on every wind,
Bring up out of that deep considering mind   90
All that you have discovered in the grave,
For it is certain that you have
Reckoned up every unforeknown, unseeing
Plunge, lured by a softening eye,
Or by a touch or a sigh,   95
Into the labyrinth of another's being;

Does the imagination dwell the most
Upon a woman won or woman lost?
If on the lost, admit you turned aside
From a great labyrinth out of pride,   100
Cowardice, some silly over-subtle thought
Or anything called conscience once;
And that if memory recur, the sun's
Under eclipse and the day blotted out.

III

It is time that I wrote my will;
I choose upstanding men
That climb the streams until
The fountain leap, and at dawn
Drop their cast at the side   5
Of dripping stone; I declare
They shall inherit my pride,
The pride of people that were
Bound neither to Cause nor to State.
Neither to slaves that were spat on,   10
Nor to the tyrants that spat,
The people of Burke and Grattan
That gave, though free to refuse –
Pride, like that of the morn,
When the headlong light is loose,   15
Or that of the fabulous horn,
Or that of the sudden shower

When all streams are dry,
Or that of the hour
When the swan must fix his eye   20
Upon a fading gleam,
Float out upon a long
Last reach of glittering stream
And there sing his last song.
And I declare my faith: 25
I mock Plotinus' thought
And cry in Plato's teeth,
Death and life were not
Till man made up the whole,
Made lock, stock and barrel   30
Out of his bitter soul,
Aye, sun and moon and star, all,
And further add to that
That, being dead, we rise,
Dream and so create   35
Translunar Paradise.
I have prepared my peace
With learned Italian things
And the proud stones of Greece,
Poet's imaginings   40
And memories of love,
Memories of the words of women,
All those things whereof
Man makes a superhuman,
Mirror-resembling dream.   45

As at the loophole there
The daws chatter and scream,
And drop twigs layer upon layer.
When they have mounted up,
The mother bird will rest   50
On their hollow top,
And so warm her wild nest.

I leave both faith and pride
To young upstanding men
Climbing the mountain-side,   55

That under bursting dawn
They may drop a fly;
Being of that metal made
Till it was broken by
This sedentary trade.   60

Now shall I make my soul,
Compelling it to study
In a learned school
Till the wreck of body,
Slow decay of blood,   65
Testy delirium
Or dull decrepitude,
Or what worse evil come—
The death of friends, or death
Of every brilliant eye   70
That made a catch in the breath—
Seem but the clouds of the sky
When the horizon fades;
Or a bird's sleepy cry
Among the deepening shades.   75

Meditations in Time of Civil War

I   ANCESTRAL HOUSES

Surely among a rich man's flowering lawns,
Amid the rustle of his planted hills,
Life overflows without ambitious pains;
And rains down life until the basin spills,
And mounts more dizzy high the more it rains   5
As though to choose whatever shape it wills
And never stoop to a mechanical
Or servile shape, at others' beck and call.

Mere dreams, mere dreams! Yet Homer had not sung
Had he not found it certain beyond dreams   10

That out of life's own self-delight had sprung
The abounding glittering jet; though now it seems
As if some marvellous empty sea-shell flung
Out of the obscure dark of the rich streams,
And not a fountain, were the symbol which   15
Shadows the inherited glory of the rich.

Some violent bitter man, some powerful man
Called architect and artist in, that they,
Bitter and violent men, might rear in stone
The sweetness that all longed for night and day,   20
The gentleness none there had ever known;
But when the master's buried mice can play,
And maybe the great-grandson of that house,
For all its bronze and marble, 's but a mouse.

O what if gardens where the peacock strays   25
With delicate feet upon old terraces,
Or else all Juno from an urn displays
Before the indifferent garden deities;
O what if levelled lawns and gravelled ways
Where slippered Contemplation finds his ease   30
And Childhood a delight for every sense,
But take our greatness with our violence?

What if the glory of escutcheoned doors,
And buildings that a haughtier age designed,
The pacing to and fro on polished floors   35
Amid great chambers and long galleries, lined
With famous portraits of our ancestors;
What if those things the greatest of mankind
Consider most to magnify, or to bless,
But take our greatness with our bitterness?   40

II   MY HOUSE

An ancient bridge, and a more ancient tower,
A farmhouse that is sheltered by its wall,
An acre of stony ground,
Where the symbolic rose can break in flower,

Old ragged elms, old thorns innumerable,   5
The sound of the rain or sound
Of every wind that blows;
The stilted water-hen
Crossing stream again
Scared by the splashing of a dozen cows;   10

A winding stair, a chamber arched with stone,
A grey stone fireplace with an open hearth,
A candle and written page.
Il Penseroso's Platonist toiled on
In some like chamber, shadowing forth   15
How the daemonic rage
Imagined everything.
Benighted travellers
From markets and from fairs
Have seen his midnight candle glimmering.   20

Two men have founded here. A man-at-arms
Gathered a score of horse and spent his days
In this tumultuous spot,
Where through long wars and sudden night alarms
His dwindlng score and he seemed castaways   15
Forgetting and forgot;
And I, that after me
My bodily heirs may find,
To exalt a lonely mind,
Befitting emblems of adversity.   30

III   MY TABLE

Two heavy trestles, and a board
Where Sato's gift, a changeless sword,
By pen and paper lies,
That it may moralise
My days out of their aimlessness.   5
A bit of an embroidered dress
Covers its wooden sheath.
Chaucer had not drawn breath
When it was forged. In Sato's house,

Curved like new moon, moon-luminous,   10
It lay five hundred years.
Yet if no change appears
No moon; only an aching heart
Conceives a changeless work of art.
Our learned men have urged   15
That when and where 'twas forged
A marvellous accomplishment,
In painting or in pottery, went
From father unto son
And through the centuries ran   20
And seemed unchanging like the sword.
Soul's beauty being most adored,
Men and their business took
The soul's unchanging look;
For the most rich inheritor,   25
Knowing that none could pass Heaven's door
That loved inferior art,
Had such an aching heart
That he, although a countrys' talk
For silken clothes and stately walk,   30
Had waking wits; it seemed
Juno's peacock screamed.

IV   MY DESCENDENTS

Having inherited a vigorous mind
From my old fathers, I must nourish dreams
And leave a woman and a man behind
As vigorous of mind, and yet it seems
Life scarce can cast a fragrance on the wind,   5
Scarce spread a glory to the morning beams,
But the torn petals strew the garden plot;
And there's but common greenness after that.

And what if my descendents lose the flower
Through natural declension of the soul,   10
Through too much business with the passing hour,
Through too much play, or marriage with a fool?
May this laborious stair and this stark tower
Become a roofless ruin that the owl

May build in the cracked masonry and cry   15
Her desolation to the desolate sky.

The Primum Mobile that fashioned us
Has made the very owls in circles move;
And I, that count myself most prosperous,
Seeing that love and friendship are enough,   20
For an old neighbour's friendship chose the house
And decked and altered it for a girl's love,
And know whatever flourish and decline
These stones remain their monument and mine.

V   THE ROAD AT MY DOOR

An affable Irregular,
A heavily-built Falstaffian man,
Comes cracking jokes of civil war
As though to die by gunshot were
The finest play under the sun.   5

A brown Lieutenant and hs men,
Half dressed in national uniform,
Stand at my door, and I complain
Of the foul weather, hail and rain,
A pear tree broken by the storm.   10

I count those feathered balls of soot
The moor-hen guides upon the stream,
To silence the envy in my thought;
And turn towards my chamber, caught
In the cold snows of a dream.   15

VI   THE STARE'S NEST BY WINDOW

The bees build in the crevices
Of loosening masonry, and there
The mother birds bring grubs and flies.
My wall is loosening; honey-bees,
Come build in the empty house of the stare.   5

We are closed in, and the key is turned
On our uncertainty; somewhere
A man is killed, or a house burned,
Yet no clear fact to be discerned:
Come build in the empty house of the stare.   10

A barricade of stone or of wood;
Some fourteen days of civil war;
Last night they trundled down the road
That dead young soldier in his blood:
Come build in the empty house of the stare.   15

We had fed the heart on fantasties,
The heart's grown brutal from the fare;
More substance in our enmities
Than in our love; O honey-bees,
Come build in the empty house of the stare.   20

VII   I SEE PHANTOMS OF HATRED AND OF THE
HEART'S FULLNESS AND OF THE COMING EMPTINESS

I climb to the tower-top and lean upon broken stone,
A mist that is like blown snow is sweeping over all,
Valley, river, and elms, under the light of a moon
That seems unlike itself, that seems unchangeable,
A glittering sword out of the east. A puff of wind   5
And those white glimmering fragments of the mist sweep by.
Frenzies bewilder, reveries perturb the mind;
Monstrous familiar images swim to the mind's eye.

'Vengeance upon the murderers,' the cry goes up,
'Vengeance for Jacques Molay.' In cloud-pale rags, or in lace,   10
The rage-driven, rage-tormented, and rage-hungry troop,
Trooper belabouring trooper, biting at arm or at face,
Plunges towards nothing, arms and fingers spreading wide
For the embrace of nothing; and I, my wits astray
Because of all that senseless tumult, all but cried   15
For vengeance on the murderers of Jacques Molay.

Their legs long, delicate and slender, aquamarine their eyes,
Magical unicorns bear ladies on their backs.

The ladies close their musing eyes. No prophecies,
Remembered out of Babylonian almanacs,   20
Have closed the ladies' eyes, their minds are but a pool
Where even longing drowns under its own excess;
Nothing but stillness can remain when hearts are full
Of their own sweetness, bodies of their loveliness.

The cloud-pale unicorns, the eyes of aquamarine,   25
The quivering half-closed eyelids, the rags of the cloud or of
    lace,
Or eyes that rage has brightened, arms it has made lean,
Give place to an indifferent multitude, give place
To brazen hawks. Nor self-delighting reverie,
Nor hate of what's to come, nor pity for what's gone,   30
Nothing but grip of claw, and the eye's complacency,
The innumberable clanging wings that have put out the
    moon.

I turn away and shut the door, and on the stair
Wonder how many times I could have proved my worth
In something that all others understand or share;   35
But O! ambitious heart, had such a proof drawn forth
A company of friends, a conscience set at ease,
It had but made us pine the more. The abstract joy,
The half-read wisdom of daemonic images,
Suffice the ageing man as once the growing boy.   40

Leda and the Swan

A sudden blow: the great wings beating still
Above the staggering girl, her thighs caressed
By the dark webs, her nape caught in his bill,
He holds her helpless breast upon his breast.

How can those terrified vague fingers push   5
The feathered glory from her loosening thighs?

And how can body, laid in that white rush,
But feel the strange heart beating where it lies?

A shudder in the loins engenders there
The broken wall, the burning roof and tower   10
And Agamemnon dead.

                        Being so caught up,
So mastered by the brute blood of the air,
Did she put on his knowledge with his power
Before the indifferent beak could let her drop?

Among School Children

I

I walk through the long schoolroom questioning;
A kind old nun in a white hood replies;
The children learn to cipher and to sing,
To study reading-books and history,
To cut and sew, be neat in everything   5
In the best modern way – the children's eyes
In momentary wonder stare upon
A sixty-year-old smiling public man.

II

I dream of a Ledaean body, bent
Above a sinking fire, a tale that she
Told of a harsh reproof, or trivial event
That changed some childish day to tragedy –
Told, and it seemed that our two natures blent   5
Into a sphere from youthful sympathy,
Or else, to alter Plato's parable,
Into the yolk and white of the one shell.

III

And thinking of that fit of grief or rage
I look upon one child or t'other there
And wonder if she stood so at that age –
For even daughters of the swan can share
Something of every paddler's heritage –   5
And had that colour upon cheek or hair,
And thereupon my heart is driven wild:
She stands before me as a living child.

IV

Her present image floats into the mind –
Did Quattrocentro finger fashion it
Hollow of cheek as though it drank the wind
And took a mess of shadows for its meat?
And I though never of Ledaean kind   5
Had pretty plumage once – enough of that,
Better to smile on all that smile, and show
There is a comfortable kind of old scarecrow.

V

What youthful mother, a shape upon her lap
Honey of generation had betrayed,
And that must sleep, shriek, struggle to escape
As recollection or the drug decide,
Would think her son, did she but see that shape   5
With sixty or more winters on its head,
A compensation for the pang of his birth,
Or the uncertainty of his setting forth?

VI

Plato thought nature but a spume that plays
Upon a ghostly paradigm of things;
Solider Aristotle played the taws
Upon the bottom of a king of kings;
World-famous golden-thighed Pythagoras   5
Fingered upon a fiddle-stick or strings

What a star sang and careless Muses heard:
Old clothes upon old sticks to scare a bird.

VII

Both nuns and mothers worship images,
But those the candles light are not as those
That animate a mother's reveries,
But keep a marble or a bronze repose.
And yet they too break hearts—O Presences   5
That passion, piety or affection knows,
And that all heavenly glory symbolise—
O self-born mockers of man's enterprise;

VIII

Labour is blossoming or dancing where
The body is not bruised to pleasure soul,
Nor beauty born out of his own despair,
Nor blear-eyed wisdom out of midnight oil.
O chestnut tree, great rooted blossomer,   5
Are you the leaf, the blossom or the bole?
O body swayed to music, O brightening glance,
How can we know the dancer from the dance?

All Souls' Night

Epilogue to 'A Vision'
Midnight has come, and the great Christ Church Bell
And may a lesser bell sound through the room;
And it is All Souls' Night,
And two long glasses brimmed with muscatel
Bubble upon the table. A ghost may come;   5
For it is a ghost's right,
His element is so fine
Being sharpened by his death,

To drink from the wine-breath
While our gross palates drink from the whole wine. 10

I need some mind that, if the cannon sound
From every quarter of the world, can stay
Wound in mind's pondering
As mummies in the mummy-cloth are wound;
Because I have a marvellous thing to say, 15
A certain marvellous thing
None but the living mock,
Though not for sober ear;
It may be all that hear
Should laugh and weep an hour upon the clock. 20

Horton's the first I call. He loved strange thought
And knew that sweet extremity of pride
That's called platonic love,
And that to such a pitch of passion wrought
Nothing could bring him, when his lady died, 25
Anodyne for his love.
Words were but wasted breath;
One dear hope had he:
The inclemency
Of that or the next winter would be death. 30

Two thoughts were so mixed up I could not tell
Whether of her or God he thought the most,
But think that his mind's eye,
When upward turned, on one sole image fell;
And that a slight companionable ghost, 35
Wild with divinity,
Had so lit up the whole
Immense miraculous house
The Bible promised us,
It seemed a gold-fish swimming in a bowl. 40

On Florence Emery I call the next,
Who finding the first wrinkles on a face
Admired and beautiful,
And knowing that the future would be vexed

With 'minished beauty, multiplied commonplace,   45
Preferred to teach a school
Away from neighbour or friend,
Among dark skins, and there
Permit foul years to wear
Hidden from eyesight to the unnoticed end.   50

Before that end much had she ravelled out
From a discourse in figurative speech
By some learned Indian
On the soul's journey. How it is whirled about,
Wherever the orbit of the moon can reach,   55
Until it plunge into the sun;
And there, free and yet fast,
Being both Chance and Choice,
Forget its broken toys
And sink into its own delight at last.   60

And I call up MacGregor from the grave,
For in my first hard springtime we were friends,
Although of late estranged.
I thought him half a lunatic, half knave,
And told him so, but friendship never ends;   65
And what if mind seem changed,
And it seem changed with the mind,
When thoughts rise up unbid
On generous things that he did
And I grow half contented to be blind!   70

He had much industry at setting out,
Much boisterous courage, before loneliness
Had driven him crazed;
For meditations upon unknown thought
Make human intercourse grow less and less;   75
They are neither paid nor praised.
But he'd object to the host,
The glass because my glass;
A ghost-lover he was
And may have grown more arrogant being a ghost.   80

But names are nothing. What matter who it be,
So that his clements have grown so fine
The fume of muscatel
Can give his sharpened palate ecstasy
No living man can drink from the whole wine.   85
I have mummy truths to tell
Whereat the living mock,
Though not for sober ear,
For maybe all that hear
Should laugh and weep an hour upon the clock.   90

Such thought – such thought have I that hold it tight
Till meditation master all its parts,
Nothing can stay my glance
Until that glance run in the world's despite
To where the damned have howled away their hearts,   95
And where the blessed dance;
Such thought, that in it bound
I need no other thing,
Wound in mind's wandering
As mummies in the mummy-cloth are wound.   100

In Memory of Eva Gore-Booth
and Con Markiewicz

The light of evening, Lissadell,
Great windows open to the south,
Two girls in silk kimonos, both
Beautiful, one a gazelle.
But a raving autumn shears   5
Blossom from the summer's wreath;
The older is condemned to death,
Pardoned, drags out lonely years
Conspiring among the ignorant.
I know not what the younger dreams—   10

Some vague Utopia—and she seems,
When withered old and skeleon-gaunt,
An image of such politics.
Many a time I think to seek
One or the other out and speak   15
Of that old Georgian mansion, mix
Pictures of the mind, recall
That table and the talk of youth,
Two girls in silk kimonos, both
Beautiful, one a gazelle.   20

Dear shadows, now you know it all,
All the folly of a fight
With a common wrong or right.
The innocent and the beautiful
Have no enemy but time;   25
Arise and bid me strike a match
And strike another till time catch;
Should the conflagration climb,
Run till all the sages know.
We the great gazebo built,   30
They convicted us of guilt;
Bid me strike a match and blow.

Death

Nor dread nor hope attend
A dying animal;
A man awaits his end
Dreading and hoping all;
Many times he died,   5
Many times rose again.
A great man in his pride
Confronting murderous men
Casts derision upon
Supersession of breath;   10

He knows death to the bone—
Man has created death.

A Dialogue of Self and Soul

I

My Soul. I summon to the winding ancient stair;
Set all your mind upon the steep ascent,
Upon the broken, crumbling battlement,
Upon the breathless starlit air,
Upon the star that marks the hidden pole;   5
Fix every wandering thought upon
That quarter where all thought is done:
Who can distinguish darkness from the soul?

My Self. The consecrated blade upon my knees
Is Sato's ancient blade, still as it was,   10
Still razor-keen, still like a looking-glass
Unspotted by the centuries;
That flowering, silken, old embroidery, torn
From some court-lady's dress and round
The wooden scabbard bound and wound,   15
Can, tattered, still protect, faded adorn.

My Soul. Why should the imagination of a man
Long past his prime remember things that are
Emblematical of love and war?
Think of ancestral night that can,   20
If but imagination scorn the earth
And intellect its wandering
To this and that and t'other thing,
Deliver from the crime of death and birth.

My Self. Montashigi, third of his family, fashioned it   25
Five hundred years ago, about it lie

Flowers from I know not what embroidery –
Heart's purple—and all these I set
For emblems of the day against the tower
Emblematical of the night,   30
And claim as by a soldier's right
A charter to commit the crime once more.

My Soul. Such fullness in that quarter overflows
And falls into the basin of the mind
That man is stricken deaf and dumb and blind,   35
For intellect no longer knows
Is from the *Ought*, or *Knower* from the *Known*—
That is to say, ascends to Heaven;
Only the dead can be forgiven;
But when I think of that my tongue's a stone.   40

II

My Self. A living man is blind and drinks his drop.
What matter if the ditches are impure?
What matter if I live it all once more?
Endure that toil of growing up;
The ignominy of boyhood; the distress   5
Of boyhood changing into man;
The unfinished man and his pain
Brought face to face with his own clumsiness;

The finished man among his enemies?—
How in the name of Heaven can he escape   10
The defiling and disfigured shape
The mirror of malicious eyes
Casts upon his eyes until at last
He thinks that shape must be his shape?
And what's the good of an escape   15
If honour find him in the wintry blast?

I am content to live it all again
And yet again, if it be life to pitch
Into the frog-spawn of a blind man's ditch,
A blind man battering blind men;

Or into that most fecund ditch of all,
The folly that man does
Or must suffer, if he woos
A proud woman not kindred of his soul.

I am content to follow to its source   25
Every event in action or in thought;
Measure the lot; forgive myself the lot!
When such as I cast out remorse
So great a sweetness flows into the breast
We must laugh and we must sing,   30
We are blest by everything,
Everything we look upon is blest.

Coole Park and Ballylee, 1931

Under my window-ledge the waters race,
Otters below and moor-hens on the top,
Run for a mile undimmed in Heaven's face
Then darkening through 'dark' Raftery's 'cellar' drop,
Run underground, rise in a rocky place   5
In Coole demesne, and there to finish up
Spread to a lake and drop into a hole.
What's water but the generated soul?

Upon the border of that lake's a wood
Now all dry sticks under a wintry sun,   10
And in a copse of beeches there I stood,
For Nature's pulled her tragic buskin on
And all the rant's a mirror of my mood:
At sudden thunder of the mounting swan
I turned about and looked where branches break   15
The glittering reaches of the flooded lake.

Another emblem there! That stormy white
But seems a concentration of the sky;
And, like the soul, it sails into the sight

And in the morning's gone, no man knows why;   20
And is so lovely that it sets to right
What knowledge or its lack had set awry,
So arrogantly pure, a child might think
It can be murdered with a spot of ink.

Sound of a stick upon the floor, a sound   25
From somebody that toils from chair to chair;
Beloved books that famous hands have bound,
Old marble heads, old pictures, everywhere;
Great rooms where travelled men and children found
Content or joy; a last inheritor   30
Where none has reigned that lacked a name and fame
Or out of folly into folly came.

A spot whereon the founders lived and died
Seemed once more dear than life; ancestral trees,
Or garden rich in memory glorified   35
Marriages, alliances and families,
And every bride's ambition satisfied.
Where fashion or mere fantasy decrees
We shift about – all that great glory spent –
Like some poor Arab tribesman and his tent.   40

We were the last romantics – chose for theme
Traditional sanctity and loveliness;
Whatever's written in what poet's name
The book of the people; whatever most can bless
The mind of man or elevate a rhyme;   45
But all is changed, that high horse riderless,
Though mounted in that saddle Homer rode
Where the swan drifts upon a darkening flood.

Swift's Epitaph

Swift has sailed into his rest;
Savage indignation there
Cannot lacerate his breast.
Imitate him if you dare,
World-besotted traveller; he   5
Served human liberty.

At Algeciras – A Meditation upon Death

The heron-billed pale cattle-birds
That feed on some foul parasite
Of the Moroccan flocks and herds
Cross the narrow Straits to light
In the rich midnight of the garden trees   5
Till the dawn break upon those mingled seas.

Often at evening when a boy
Would I carry to a friend—
Hoping more substantial joy
Did an older mind commend—   10
Not such as are in Newton's metaphor,
But actual shells of Rosses' level shore.

Greater glory in the Sun,
An evening chill upon the air,
Bid imagination run   15
Much on the Great Questioner;
What He can question, what if questioned I
Can with a fitting confidence reply.

The Choice

The intellect of man is forced to choose
Perfection of the life, or of the work,
And if it take the second must refuse
A heavenly mansion, raging in the dark.
When all that story's finished, what's the news?   5
In luck or out the toil has left its mark:
That old perplexity an empty purse,
Or the day's vanity, the night's remorse.

Byzantium

The unpurged images of day recede;
The Emperor's drunken soldiery are abed;
Night resonance recedes, night walkers' song
After great cathedral gong;
A starlit or a moonlit dome disdains   5
All that man is,
All mere complexities,
The fury and the mire of human veins.

Before me floats an image, man or shade,
Shade more than man, more image than a shade;   10
For Hades' bobbin bound in mummy-cloth
May unwind the winding path;
A mouth that has no moisture and no breath
Breathless mouths may summon;
I hail the superhuman;   15
I call it death-in-life and life-in-death.

Miracle, bird or golden handiwork,
More miracle than bird or handiwork,
Planted on the star-lit golden bough,
Can like the cocks of Hades crow,   20

Or, by the moon embittered, scorn aloud
In glory of changless metal
Common bird or petal
And all complexities of mire or blood.

At midnight on the Emperor's pavement flit   25
Flames that no faggot feeds, nor steel has lit,
Nor storm disturbs, flames begotten of flame,
Where blood-begotten spirits come
And all complexities of fury leave,
Dying into a dance,   30
An agony of trance,
An agony of flame that cannot singe a sleeve.

Astraddle on the dolphin's mire and blood,
Spirit after spirit! The smithies break the flood,
The golden smithies of the Emperor!   35
Marbles of the dancing floor
Break bitter furies of complexity,
Those images that yet
Fresh images beget,
That dolphin-torn, that gong-tormented sea.   40

Vacillation

I

Between extremities
Man runs his course;
A brand, or flaming breath,
Comes to destroy
All those antinomies   5
Of day and night;
The body calls it death,
The heart remorse.
But if these be right
What is joy?

II

A tree there is that from its topmost bough
Is half all glittering flame and half all green
Abounding foliage moistened with the dew;
And half is half and yet is all the scene;
And half and half consume what they renew,   5
And he that Attis' image hangs between
That staring fury and the blind lush leaf
May know not what he knows, but knows not grief.

III

Get all the gold and silver that you can,
Satisfy ambition, or animate
The trivial days and ram them with the sun,
And yet upon these maxims meditate:
All women dote upon an idle man   5
Although their children need a rich estate;
No man has ever lived that had enough
Of children's gratitude or woman's love.

No longer in Lethean foliage caught   10
Begin the preparation for your death
And from the fortieth winter by that thought
Test every work of intellect or faith,
And everything that your own hands have wrought,
And call those works extravagance of breath
That are not suited for such men as come   15
Proud, open-eyed and laughing to the tomb.

IV

My fiftieth year had come and gone,
I sat, a solitary man,
In a crowded London shop,
An open book and empty cup
On the marble table-top   5

While on the shop and street I gazed
My body of a sudden blazed;

And twenty minutes more or less
It seemed, so great my happiness,
That I was blessèd and could bless.   10

V

Although the summer sunlight gild
Cloudy leafage of the sky,
On wintry moonlight sink the field
In storm-scattered intricacy,
I cannot look thereon,   5
Responsibility so weighs me down

Things said or done long years ago,
Or things I did not do or say
But thought that I might say or do,
Weigh me down, and not a day   10
But something is recalled,
My conscience or my vanity appalled.

VI

A rivery field spread out below,
An odour of the new-mown hay
In his nostrils, the great lord of Chou
Cried, casting off the mountain snow,
'Let all things pass away.'   5

Wheels by milk-white asses drawn
Where Babylon or Nineveh
Rose; some conqueror drew rein
And cried to battle-weary men,
'Let all things pass away.'   10

From man's blood-sodden heart are sprung
Those branches of the night and day
Where the gaudy moon is hung.
What's the meaning of all song?
'Let all things pass away.'   15

VII

The Soul. Seek out reality, leave things that seem.
The Heart. What, be a singer born and lack a theme?
The Soul. Isaiah's coal, what more can man desire?
The Heart. Struck dumb in the simplicity of fire!
The Soul. Look on that fire, salvation walks within.   5
The Heart. What theme had Homer but original sin?

VIII

Must we part, Von Hügel, though much alike, for we
Accept the miracles of the saints and honour sanctity?
The body of Saint Teresa lies undecayed in tomb,
Bathed in miraculous oil, sweet odours from it come,
Healing from its lettered slab. Those self-same hands
    perchance   5
Eternalised the body of a modern saint that once
Had scooped out Pharoah's mummy. I – though heart might
    find relief
Did I become a Christian man and choose for my belief
What seems most welcome in the tomb – play a predestined
    part.
Homer is my example and his unchristened heart.   10
The lion and the honeycomb, what has Scriptures said?
So get you gone, Von Hügel, though with blessings on your
    head.

Remorse for Intemperate Speech

I ranted to the knave and fool,
But outgrew that school,
Would transform the part,
Fit audience found, but cannot rule
My fanatic heart.   5

I sought my betters: though in each
Fine manners, liberal speech,
Turn hatred into sport,
Nothing said or done can reach
My fanatic heart.   10

Out of Ireland have we come.
Great hatred, little room,
Maimed us at the start.
I carry from my mother's womb
A fanatic heart.   15

Stream and Sun at Glendalough

Through intricate motions ran
Stream and gliding sun
And all my heart seemed gay:
Some stupid thing that I had done
Made my attention stray.   5

Repentance keeps my heart impure;
But what am I that dare
Fancy that I can
Better conduct myself or have more
Sense than a common man?

What motion of the sun or stream
Or eyelid shot the gleam
That pierced my body through?
What made me live like these that seem
Self-born, born anew?   15

Crazy Jane talks with the Bishop

I met the Bishop on the road
And much said he and I,
'Those breasts are flat and fallen now,
Those veins must soon be dry;
Live in a heavenly mansion,   5
Not in some foul sty.'

'Fair and foul are near of kin,
And fair needs foul,' I cried.
'My friends are gone, but that's a truth
Nor grave nor bed denied,   10
Learned in bodily lowliness
And in the heart's pride.

'A woman can be proud and stiff
When on love intent;
But Love has pitched his mansion in   15
The place of excrement;
For nothing can be sole or whole
That has not been rent.'

After Long Silence

Speech after long silence; it is right,
All other lovers being estranged or dead,
Unfriendly lamplight hid under its shade,
The curtains drawn upon unfriendly night,
That we descant and yet again descant   5
Upon the supreme theme of Art and Song:
Bodily decreptitude is wisdom; young
We loved each other and were ignorant.

Her Vision in the Wood

Dry timber under that rich foliage,
At wine-dark midnight in the sacred wood,
Too old for a man's love I stood in rage
Imagining men. Imagining that I could
A greater with a lesser pang assuage   5
Or but to find if withered vein ran blood,
I tore my body that its wine might cover
Whatever could recall the lip of lover.

And after that I held my fingers up,
Stared at the wine-dark nail, or dark that ran   10
Down every withered finger from the top;
But the dark changed to red, and torches shone,
And deafening music shook the leaves; a troop
Shouldered a litter with a wounded man,
Or smote upon the string and to the sound   15
Sang of the beast that gave the fatal wound.

All stately women moving to a song
With loosened hair or foreheads grief-distraught,
It seemed a Quattrocento painter's throng,
A thoughtless image of Mantegna's thought –   20
Why should they think that are for ever young?
Till suddenly in grief's contagion caught,
I stared upon his blood-bedabbled breast
And sang my malediction with the rest.

That thing all blood and mire, that beast-torn wreck,   25
Half turned and fixed a glazing eye on mine,
And, though love's bitter-sweet had all come back,
Those bodies from a picture or a coin
Nor saw my body fall nor heard it shriek,
Nor knew, drunken with singing as with wine,   30
That they had brought no fabulous symbol there
But my heart's victim and its torturer.

A Prayer for Old Age

God guard me from those thoughts men think
In the mind alone;
He that sings a lasting song
Thinks in a marrow-bone;

From all that makes a wise old man
That can be praised of all;
O what am I that I should not seem
For the song's sake a fool?

I pray – for fashion's word is out
And prayer comes round again –
That I may seem, though I die old,
A foolish, passionate man.

Meru

Civilisation is hooped together, brought
Under a rule, under the semblance of peace
By manifold illusion; but man's life is thought,
And he, despite his terror, cannot cease
Ravening through century after century,   5
Ravening, raging, and uprooting that he may come
Into the desolation of reality:
Egypt and Greece, good-bye, and good-bye, Rome!
Hermits upon Mount Meru or Everest,
Caverned in night under the drifted snow,   10
Or where that snow and winter's dreadful blast
Beat down upon their naked bodies, know
That day brings round the night, that before dawn
His glory and his monuments are gone.

The Gyres

The gyres! the gyres! Old Rocky Face, look forth;
Things thought too long can be no longer thought,
For beauty dies of beauty, worth of worth,
And ancient lineaments are blotted out.
Irrational streams of blood are staining earth;   5
Empedocles has thrown all things about;
Hector is dead and there's a light in Troy;
We that look on but laugh in tragic joy.

What matter though numb nightmare ride on top,
And blood and mire the sensitive body stain?   10
What matter? Heave no sigh, let no tear drop,
A greater, a more gracious time has gone;
For painted forms or boxes of make-up
In ancient tombs I sighed, but not again;
What matter? Our of cavern come a voice,   15
And all it knows is that one word 'Rejoice!'

Conduct and work grow coarse, and coarse the soul,
What matter? Those that Rocky Face holds dear,
Lovers of horses and of women, shall,
From marble of a broken sepulchre,   20
Or dark betwixt the polecat and the owl,
Or any rich, dark nothing disinter
The workman, noble and saint, and all things run
On that unfashionable gyre again.

Lapis Lazuli

(For Harry Clifton)

I have heard that hysterical women say
They are sick of the palette and fiddle-bow,
Of poets that are always gay,
For everybody knows or else should know
That if nothing drastic is done   5
Aeroplane and Zeppelin will come out,
Pitch like King Billy bomb-balls in
Until the town lie beaten flat.

All perform their tragic play,
There struts Hamlet, there is Lear,   10
That's Ophelia, that Cordelia;
Yet they, should the last scene be there,
The great stage curtain about to drop,
If worthy their prominent part in the play,
Do not break up their lives to weep.   15
They know that Hamlet and Lear are gay;
Gaiety transfiguring all that dread.
All men have aimed at, found and lost;
Black out; Heaven blazing into the head:
Tragedy wrought to its uttermost.   20
Though Hamlet rambles and Lear rages,
And all the drop-scenes drop at once
Upon a hundred thousand stages,
It cannot grow by an inch or an ounce.

On their own feet they came, or on shipboard,   25
Camel-back, horse-back, ass-back, mule-back,
Old civilisations put to the sword.
Then they and their wisdom went to rack:
No handiwork of Callimachus,
Who handled marble as if it were bronze,   30
Made draperies that seemed to rise
When sea-wind swept the corner, stands;

His long lamp-chimney shaped like the stem
Of a slender palm, stood but a day;
All things fall and are built again,   35
And those that build them again are gay.

Two Chinamen, behind them a third,
Are carved in lapis lazuli,
Over them flies a long-legged bird,
A symbol of longevity;   40
The third, doubtless a serving-man,
Carries a musical instrument.

Every discoloration of the stone,
Every accidental crack or dent,
Seems a water-course or an avalanche,   45
Or lofty slope where it still snows
Though doubtless plum or cherry-branch
Sweetens the little half-way house
Those Chinamen climb towards, and I
Delight to imagine them seated there;   50
There, on the mountain and the sky,
On all the tragic scene they stare.
One asks for mournful melodies;
Accomplished fingers begin to play.
Their eyes mid many wrinkles, their eyes,   55
Their ancient, glittering eyes, are gay.

An Acre of Grass

Picture and book remain,
An acre of green grass
For air and exercise,
Now strength of body goes;
Midnight, an old house   5
Where nothing stirs but a mouse.

My temptation is quiet.
Here at life's end
Neither loose imagination,
Nor the mill of the mind   10
Consuming its rag and bone,
Can make the truth known.

Grant me an old man's frenzy,
Myself must I remake
Till I am Timon and Lear   15
Or that William Blake
Who beat upon the wall
Till Truth obeyed his call;

A mind Michael Angelo knew
That can pierce the clouds,   20
Or inspired by frenzy
Shake the dead in their shrouds;
Forgotten else by mankind,
An old man's eagle mind.

What Then?

His chosen comrades thought at school
He must grow a famous man;
He thought the same and lived by rule,
All his twenties crammed with toil;
'What then?' sang Plato's ghost. 'What then?'   5

Everything he wrote was read,
After certain years he won
Sufficient money for his need,
Friends that have been friends indeed;
'What then?' sang Plato's ghost. 'What then?'   10

All his happier dreams came true –
A small old house, wife, daughter, son,

Grounds where plum and cabbage grew,
Poets and Wits about him drew;
'What then?' sang Plato's ghost. 'What then?'   15

'The work is done,' grown old he thought,
'According to my boyish plan;
Let the fools rage, I swerved in naught,
Something to perfection brought';
But louder sang that ghost, 'What then?'   20

The Curse of Cromwell

You ask what I have found, and far and wide I go:
Nothing but Cromwell's house and Cromwell's murderous
    crew,
The lovers and the dancers are beaten into the clay,
And the tall men and the swordsmen and the horsemen,
    where are they?
And there is an old beggar wandering in his pride—   5
His fathers served their fathers before Christ was crucified.
         O what of that, O what of that,
          What is there left to say?

All neighbourly content and easy talk are gone,
But there's no good complaining, for money's rant is on.   10
He that's mounting up must on his neighbour mount,
And we and all the Muses are things of no account.
They have schooling of their own, but I pass their schooling
    by,
What can they know that we know that know the time to die?
         O what of that, O what of that,   15
          What is there left to say?

But there's another knowledge that my heart destroys,
As the fox in the old fable destroyed the Spartan boy's,

Because it proves that things both can and cannot be;
That the swordsmen and the ladies can still keep company,   5
Can pay the poet for a verse and hear the fiddle sound,
That I am still their servant though all are underground.
                    O what of that, O what of that,
                    What is there left to say?

I came on a great house in the middle of the night,   25
Its open lighted doorway and its windows all alight,
And all my friends were there and made me welcome too;
But I woke in an old ruin that the winds howled through;
And when I pay attention I must out and walk
Among the dogs and horses that understand my talk.   30
                    O what of that, O what of that,
                    What is there left to say?

The Spur

You think it horrible that lust and rage
Should dance attention upon my old age;
They were not such a plague when I was young;
What else have I to spur me into song?

Why Should not old Men be Mad?

Why should not old men be mad?
Some have known a likely lad
That had a sound fly-fisher's wrist
Turn to a drunken journalist;
A girl that knew all Dante once   5
Live to bear children to a dunce;
A Helen of social welfare dream,

Climb on a wagonette to scream.
Some think it a matter of course that chance
Should starve good men and bad advance,   10
That if their neighbours figured plain,
As though upon a lighted screen,
No single story would they find
Of an unbroken happy mind,
A finish worthy of the start.   15
Young men know nothing of this sort,
Observant old men know it well;
And when they know what old books tell,
And that no better can be had,
Know why an old man should be mad.   20

The Statues

Pythagoras planned it. Why did the people stare?
His numbers, though they moved to seemed to move
In marble or in bronze, lacked character.
But boys and girls, pale from the imagined love
Of solitary beds, knew what they were,   5
That passion could bring character enough,
And pressed at midnight in some public place
Live lips upon a plummet-measured face.

No! Greater than Pythagoras, for the men
That with a mallet or a chisel modelled these   10
Calculations that look but casual flesh, put down
All Asiatic vague immensities,
And not the banks of oars that swam upon
That many-headed foam at Salamis
Europe put off that foam when Phidias   15
Gave women dreams and dreams their looking-glass.

One image crossed the many-headed, sat
Under the tropic shade, grew round and slow,

No Hamlet thin from eating flies, a fat
Dreamer of the Middle Ages. Empty eyeballs knew   20
That knowledge increases unreality, that
Mirror on mirror mirrored is all the show.
When gong and conch declare the hour to bless
Grimalkin crawls to Buddha's emptiness.

When Pearse summoned Cuchulain to his side,   25
What stalked through the Post Office? What intellect,
What calculation, number, measurement, replied?
We Irish, born into that ancient sect
But thrown upon this filthy modern tide
And by its formless spawning fury wrecked,   30
Climb to our proper dark, that we may trace
The lineaments of a plummet-measured face.

Long-Legged Fly

That civilisation may not sink,
Its great battle lost,
Quiet the dog, tether the pony
To a distant post;
Our master Caesar is in the tent   5
Where the maps are spread,
His eyes fixed upon nothing,
A hand under his head.

Like a long-legged fly upon the stream
His mind moves upon silence.   10

That the topless towers be burnt
And men recall that face,
Move most gently if move you must
In this lonely place.
She thinks, part woman, three parts a child,   15
That nobody looks; her feet

Practise a tinker shuffle
Picked up on a street.

Like a long-legged fly upon the stream
Her mind moves upon silence   20

That girls at puberty may find
The first Adam in their thought,
Shut the door of the Pope's chapel,
Keep those children out.
There on that scaffolding reclines   25
Michael Angelo.
With no more sound than the mice make
His hand moves to and fro.

Like a long-legged fly upon the stream
His mind moves upon silence.   30

A Bronze Head

Here at right of the entrance this bronze head,
Human, superhuman, a bird's round eye,
Everything else withered and mummy-dead.
What great tomb-haunter sweeps the distant sky
(Something may linger there though all else die;)   5
And finds there nothing to make its terror less
Hysteria passio of its own emptiness?

No dark tomb-haunter once; her form all full
As though with magnanimity of light,
Yet a most gentle woman; who can tell   10
Which of her forms has shown her substance right?
Or maybe substance can be composite,
Profound McTaggart thought so, and in a breath
A mouthful held the extreme of life and death.

But even at the starting-post, all sleek and new,   15
I saw the wildness in her and I thought
A vision of terror that it must live through
Had shattered her soul. Propinquity had brought
Imagination to that pitch where it casts out
All that is not iself: I had grown wild   20
And wandered murmuring everywhere, 'My child, my child!'

Or else I thought her supernatural;
As though a sterner eye looked through her eye
On this foul world in its decline and fall;
On gangling stocks grown great, great stocks run dry,   25
Ancestral pearls all pitched into a sty,
Heroic reverie mocked by clown and knave,
And wondered what was left for massacre to save.

The Man and the Echo

Man
In a cleft that's christened Alt
Under broken stone I halt
At the bottom of a pit
That broad noon has never lit,
And shout a secret to the stone.   5
All that I have said and done,
Now that I am old and ill,
Turns into a question till
I lie awake night after night
And never get the answers right.   10
Did that play of mine send out
Certain men the English shot?
Did words of mine put too great strain
On that woman's reeling brain?
Could my spoken words have checked   15
That whereby a house lay wrecked?
And all seems evil until I

Sleepless would lie down and die.

Echo
Lie down and die.

Man
                        That were to shirk
The spiritual intellect's great work,   20
And shirk it in vain. There is no release
In a bodkin or disease,
Nor can there be work so great
As that which cleans man's dirty slate.
While man can still his body keep   25
Wine or love drug him to sleep,
Waking he thanks the Lord that he
Has body and its stupidity,
But body gone he sleeps no more,
And till his intellect grow sure   30
That all's arranged in one clear view,
Pursues the thoughts that I pursue,
Then stands in judgment on his soul,
And, all work done, dismisses all
Out of intellect and sight   35
And sinks at last into the night

Echo
Into the night.

Man
                        O Rocky Voice,
Shall we in that great night rejoice?
What do we know but that we face
One another in this place?   40
But hush, for I have lost the theme,
Its joy or night seem but a dream;
Up there some hawk or owl has struck,
Dropping out of sky or rock,
A stricken rabbit is crying out,   45
And its cry distracts my thought.

The Circus Animals' Desertion

I

I sought a theme and sought for it in vain,
I sought it daily for six weeks or so.
Maybe at last, being but a broken man,
I must be satisfied with my heart, although
Winter and summer till old age began   5
My circus animals were all on show,
Those stilted boys, that burnished chariot,
Lion and woman and the Lord knows what.

II

What can I but enumerate old themes?
First that sea-rider Oisin led by the nose
Through three enchanted islands, allegorical dreams,
Vain gaiety, vain battle, vain repose,
Themes of the embittered heart, or so it seems,   5
That might adorn old songs or courtly shows;
But what cared I that set him on to ride,
I, starved for the bosom of his faery bride?

And then a counter-truth filled out its play,
The Countess Cathleen was the name I gave it;   10
She, pity-crazed, had given her soul away,
But masterful Heaven had intervened to save it.
I thought my dear must her own soul destroy,
So did fanaticism and hate enslave it,
And this brought forth a dream and soon enough   15
This dream itself had all my thought and love.

And when the Fool and Blind Man stole the bread
Cuchulian fought the ungovernable sea;
Heart-mysteries there, and yet when all is said
It was the dream itself enchanted me: 20
Character isolated by a deed
To engross the present and dominate memory.
Players and painted stage took all my love,
And not those things that they were emblems of.

III

Those masterful images because complete
Grew in pure mind, but out of what began?
A mound of refuse or the sweepings of a street,
Old kettles, old bottles, and a broken can,
Old iron, old bones, old rags, that raving slut   5
Who keeps the till. Now that my ladder's gone,
I must lie down where all the ladders start,
In the foul rag-and-bone shop of the heart.

Politics

How can I, that girl standing there,
My attention fix
On Roman or on Russian
Or on Spanish politics?
Yet here's a travelled man that knows   5
What he talks about,
And there's a politician
That has read and thought,
And maybe what they say is true
Of war and war's alarms   10
But O that I were young again
And held her in my arms.

From Under Ben Bulben

V

Irish poets, learn your trade,
Sing whatever is well made,
Scorn the sort now growing up
All out of shape from toe to top,

Their unremembering hearts and heads   5
Base-born products of base beds.
Sing the peasantry, and then
Hard-riding country gentlemen,
The holiness of monks, and after
Porter-drinkers' randy laugher;   10
Sing the lords and ladies gay
That were beaten into the clay
Through seven heroic centuries;
Cast your mind on other days
That we in coming days may be   15
Still the indomitable Irishry.

VI

Under bare Ben Bulben's head
In Drumcliff churchyard Yeats is laid.
An ancestor was rector there
Long years ago, a church stands near,
By the road an ancient cross.   5
No marble, no conventional phrase;
On limestone quarried near the spot
By his command these words are cut:
      Cast a cold eye
      On life, on death.
      Horseman, pass by!   10

Notes

p. 3 *The Stolen Child*: **Sleuth Wood,** 'Wood on the Slope' on shore of Lough Gill, Co. Sligo; **Rosses,** seashore near Sligo and according to Yeats a 'noted fairy locality'; **Glen-Car,** a lake in a glen of the same name near Sligo. **p. 4** *Down by the Salley Gardens*: **salley,** willow. **p. 5** *To the Rose upon the Rood of Time*: **Rose,** a recurrent symbol in Irish poetry and in religious and mystical iconography; **Rood,** a cross (the conjunction of rose and cross was a central symbol in the Rosicrucian Order of the Golden Dawn, to which Yeats belonged); **Cuchulain,** the paramount hero of Irish mythology, was bewitched by Druids into fighting the tide after unwittingly killing his only son; **Fergus,** mythological Irish king, who according to some sources gave up his crown for the contemplative life. **p. 5** *The Lake Isle of Innisfree*: **Innisfree**; small island (literally 'Heather Island') in Lough Gill near Sligo; **wattles,** interlaced rods and twigs; **purple glow,** caused by the reflection of heather in the water. **p. 6** *The Sorrow of Love*: **Odysseus,** resourceful Greek king, whose ten-year difficulties in returning to Ithaca after the Trojan War are the subject of Homer's *Odyssey*; **Priam,** aged King of Troy, killed when the Greeks took the city. **p. 7** *When You are Old:* based on a poem by the French sixteenth-century poet Ronsard. **p. 7** *Who Goes with Fergus:* first written for the play *The Countess Cathleen*. **p. 8** *The Man who Dreamed of Faeryland:* Drumahair, village in Co. Leitrim; **Lissadell,** area north-west of Sligo; **Scanavin,** village south of Sligo; **Lugnagall,** 'Place of the Strangers', a grey cliff overlooking Glen-Car lake near Sligo. **p. 9** *To Ireland in the Coming Times*: **rann,** verse; **Davis, Mangan, Ferguson,** the best known Irish poets of the mid- and late nineteenth century. **p. 11** *The Hosting of the Sidhe*: **Sidhe,** supernatural beings in Irish myth and folklore, often associated with the wind; **Knocknarea,** mountain near Sligo on which Queen Maeve is said to be buried; **Clooth-na-Bare,** the old woman of Bare, a passionate elemental woman who drowned her fairy life in Lough Ia in Co. Sligo; **Caoilte,** a Fenian warrior who appeared to Finn in flames that he might lead him through the darkness of a forest; **Niamh,** daughter of Aengus, Irish God of Love, who carried Oisin to three enchanted islands. **p. 12** *The Song of Wandering Aengus*: original entitled 'A Mad Song'; **Aengus,** name of the Celtic god of love and music, but here a personification of the poet; **apple blossom,** Yeats associated Maud Gonne with apple blossom. **p. 13** *He bids his Beloved be at Peace*: Yeats follows tradition in associating the North with night and sleep, the East with hope, the South with passion and desire, and the West with fading and dreaming; **beloved,** Olivia Shakespear (1867–1938), with whom Yeats had an affair 1895–7, and who remained a close friend for life. **p. 14** *The Valley of the Black Pig*: the supposed site of a future Irish battle for freedom, but Yeats also saw the clash as the autumnal contest in which winter defeats summer; **cromlech,** ancient Irish constructions of stone; **cairn,** stones marking ancient burial places. **p. 14** *The Secret Rose*: **Magi,** the three Wise Men who visited the infant Jesus; **the king,** Conchubar, King of Ulster who in some accounts dies of rage after seeing a vision of Christ's crucifixion (the 'Pierced Hands') through Druid art; **Fand,** wife of the Irish Sea God, Manannan MacLir, who fell in love with the hero Cuchulain; **him who drove,** Caoilte (see above); **liss,** a fort. Caoilte performed this feat after most of his companion Red Branch Knights had been killed at the Battle of Gabhra; **barrows,** ancient burial mounds; **dreaming king,** Fergus (see above); **him who sold tillage,** a young man in a folk-story who, finding a lock of hair which shone brighter than any candle, travelled far and wide until he found the woman to whom it belonged. **p. 16** *The Fiddler of Dooney:* the names are of places near Sligo: **Dooney,** a rock near the shore of Lough Gill; **Kilvarnet,** 'the church in the gap', a townland in Co. Sligo; **Mochara-buiee,** 'the yellow plain', a townland to the south-west of Sligo. **p. 16** *In the Seven Woods*: **Seven Woods,** on Lady Gregory's Coole estate; **Tara,** in Co. Meath, ancient capital of Irish High Kings. Yeats helped to stop excavations there in 1902; **crown,** Edward VII, notorious for his sexual promiscuity, succeeded Victoria in 1901; **paper flowers,** decorations for Edward's coronation; **Great Archer,** Sagittarius, and here a symbol of relevation; **Pairc-na-Lee,** 'field of the calves', one of the seven woods of Coole. **p. 17** *The Folly of Being Comforted*: **ever kind,** probably Lady Gregory; **well-beloved,** Maud Gonne. **p. 18** *Adam's Curse*: **Curse,** original sin, caused by Adam's eating of the fruit of knowledge: see Genesis 3: 1–19; **beautiful mild woman,** Kathleen Pilcher, Maud Gonne's sister; **you,** Maud Gonne. **p. 21** *Pardon, old fathers . . .* : **Old Dublin merchant,** Benjamin Yeats (1750–95), wholesale linen merchant and Yeats's great-great-grandfather; **free of the ten and four,** as a substantial wholesale merchant not liable to customs duties of 10% on wine and tobacco and 6% (not 4%) on other goods; **country scholar,** Yeats's great-grandfather, the Revd. John Yeats (1774–1846), Rector of Drumcliffe, Co. Sligo; **Robert Emmet** (1778–1803), an Irish patriot hanged after an abortive rebellion in 1803; **Butler,** Yeats was proud of his connection with the aristocratic Ormonde family through Benjamin Yeats's marriage to Mary Butler in 1773; **an Armstrong,** one of a family with strong military traditions, which had married into the Yeatses in the late C18th; **Boyne,** the Protestant William III defeated the Catholic James II at the Battle of the Boyne in 1690, so laying the foundations for a Protestant hegemony in Ireland; **merchant skipper,** William Middleton (1770–1832), Yeats's maternal great-grandfather; **fierce old man,** William Pollexfen (1811–92), Yeats's maternal grandfather; **barren passion's sake,** Yeats's unsuccessful wooing of Maud Gonne. **p. 22 To a Wealthy Man . . . :** occasioned by Hugh Lane's unsuccessful appeal for a gallery to house the French paintings he intended to present to Dublin; **Wealthy Man,** Arthur Edward Guinness, first Baron Ardilaun (1840–1915); **Paudeen,** disparaging diminutive of Patrick and used here with 'Bridget' to represent the philistine common people; **Duke Ercole,** Ercole d'Este (1431–1505), Duke of Ferrara and patron of the arts; **Plautus,** Latin comic dramatist (c. 254–184 BC), whose plays Ercole revived; **Guidobaldo,** Guidobaldo di Montefeltro (1472–1508), Duke of Urbino, an Italian city-state celebrated for its culture and elegance by Castiglione in The Book of the Courtier; **Cosimo,** Cosimo de' Medici (1389–1464), started the great Medici tradition of patronage of the arts. He was exiled for a year (1433–4) in Venice; **Michelozzo,** Michelozzo de Bartolommeo Michelozzi (1396–1472), architect to Cosimo de' Medici; **the sun's eye,** proverbially, eagles can gaze at the sun without blinking. **p. 23 September 1913:** this poem was also inspired by the dispute over the Lane art gallery; **you,** Irish philistines; **O'Leary,** the Fenian John O'Leary (1830–1907) had deeply influenced Yeats through his austere idealism and cultural nationalism on his return from exile in 1885; **wild geese,** C18th soldiers, smuggled out of Ireland to fight for European powers; **Edward Fitzgerald,** an Irish patriot (1763–98) fatally wounded while resisting arrest; **Emmet,** see above; **Wolfe Tone,** Theobold Wolfe Tone (1763–98), leader of the United Irishmen, who committed suicide after his capture by British forces. **p. 24 Friends: One because no thought,** Olivia Shakespear (see above); **one because her hand,** Lady Augusta Gregory (1852–1932), Irish folklorist and playwright, was Yeats's closest friend, patron and correspondent from 1897 when he began to spend his summers at her house, Coole Park, in County Galway; **her,** Maud Gonne. **p. 26 The Magi:** the poem proposes that the Three Wise Men, who attended on the birth of Christ (see above), were unsatisfied by his incarnation, which ended in his crucifixion on the hill of Calvary, outside Jerusalem; **uncontrollable mystery,** the

Magi seek the incarnation of a new force, out of men's control; **bestial floor**, of the stable where Christ was born in Bethlehem. **p. 26** *While I, from that reed-throated whisperer:* poetic inspiration; **Ben Jonson's phase**, appears in *The Poetaster* (1602) by the English playwright Ben Johnson (1572–1637); 'There's something come into my thought / That must and shall be sung high and aloof, / Safe from the wolf's black jaw, and the dull ass's hoof; **Kyle-na-no**, 'Wood of the Nuts', one of the seven woods of Coole; **ancient roof**, Coole Park; **dog's defile**, according to Yeats, he took this image from the Dutch humanist Erasmus (*c.* 1466–1536). **p. 28** *In Memory of Major Robert Gregory:* Lady Gregory's only son (1881–1918), who had trained as an artist at the Slade, was shot down over Italy on 23 January 1918 while serving in the Royal Air Corps; **our house**, although Yeats wrote this poem in Ballinamantane House, a temporary home, the setting is Thoor Ballylee, the Norman Tower he had purchased in 1917. The Yeatses moved into the refurbished Tower three months after the poem was finished; **turf**, peat; **Lionel Johnson**, the poet and critic (1867–1902) who had been one of Yeats's closest London friends in the early 1890s; **much falling**, from religious grace, but the alcoholic Johnson was also reputed to have died after falling from a bar-stool; **John Synge**, Irish dramatist and poet (1871–1909), whom Yeats had met in Paris in 1897, and whom he hailed as the great Irish playwright. Synge was afflicted with chronic bad health; **stony place**, the Aran Islands off the Galway coast, to which Synge made many visits and which he describes in *The Aran Islands* (1906); **George Pollexfen**, Yeats's maternal uncle (1839–1910), businessman, astrologer, hypochondriac, and, in his youth, an accomplished horseman; **opposition, square and trine,** astrological terms, describing heavenly bodies at angles of 180°, 90°, and 120° to each other; **our Sidney,** Sir Philip Sidney (1554–86) English renaissance poet, writer, courtier, and soldier; **Castle Taylor,** a big house near Craughwell, Co. Galway, belonging to Lady Gregory's family; **Roxborough,** Lady Gregory's home before marriage, and situated between Gort and Loughrea; **Esserkelly,** near Ardrahan in Co. Galway; **Mooneen,** 'the little bog', near Esserkelly. **p. 31** *An Irish Airman*: **Kiltartan Cross,** a crossroads near Coole. Lady Gregory used the Kiltartan dialect in many of her works. **p. 34** *A Deep-sworn Vow*: **vow,** Yeats believed that he and Maud Gonne had contracted a 'mystical marriage' in the 1890s. **p. 34** *Michael Robartes and the Dancer*: **Robartes,** a magician and unruly mystic, invented by Yeats to articulate that aspect of his own character; **this altar-piece,** probably that of 'Saint George and the Dragon' in the National Gallery, Dublin; **Athene,** Pallas Athene, Greek goddess of learning; **Paul**

Veronese, name given to the Verona-born Paulo Caliari (1528–88), who painted in Venice (hence 'lagoon'), and whose large workshop included three of his sons; **Michael Angelo,** Italian artist Michelangelo Buonarroti (1475–1564), who painted the ceiling of the Sistine Chapel in the Vatican; **'Morning' and 'Night',** two celebrated sculptures in the Medici Chapel in Florence; **wine and bread,** a reference to Christ's Last Supper and the eucharist; **this Latin text,** probably an imaginary authority, although a reference to Ficino's Latin translation of Plotinus has been suggested.

p. 36 *Easter 1916*: Rising, the Easter Rising took place in central Dublin from 24 to 29 April 1916, when several hundred Republicans seized strategic buildings and fought off British troops. After their surrender, fifteen of the leaders were court-martialled and shot; **them,** the rebels-to-be; **motley,** clown's costume; **that woman,** Constance Markiewicz (née Gore-Booth, 1868–1927), born at Lissadell, Co. Sligo, whom Yeats had known since 1894. Her death sentence was commuted; **kept a school,** Patrick Pearse (1879–1916), founder of St. Enda's School (to which Yeats had lectured), and a leader of the Rising; **wingèd horse,** Pegasus, the muses' horse. Pearse was also a poet and playwright; **This other,** Thomas MacDonagh (1876–1916), poet, dramatist, and critic, whom Yeats had advised on his poetry and plays; **This other man,** John MacBride (1865–1916), who had fought for the Boers, and who married Maud Gonne in 1903; **most bitter wrong,** MacBride was alleged to have treated Maud Gonne badly, and to have sexually assaulted her daughter and step-sister. The marriage ended after less than two years; **England may keep faith,** a Home Rule Bill had been passed in 1913, but was suspended when World War I was declared; **Connolly,** James Connolly (1870–1916), a labour leader and military commander of the Rising. **p. 38 *On a Political Prisoner*:** Constance Markiewicz (see above) had been amnestied in 1917, but was imprisoned again in 1918 for sedition; **Ben Bulben,** a mountain overlooking Sligo and close to Lissadell, Con Markiewicz's childhood home.

p. 39 *The Second Coming*: takes its theme from Christ's prediction of the Second Coming (Matthew: 24) and St. John's description of the Beast of the Apocalypse (Revelation); **widening gyre,** Yeats conceived of History as two spinning interlocking cones. When an epoch arrives at the base of one cone, there is a sudden reversal, and a new dispensation begins. Yeats believed that the Christian period was drawing to a close, and an antithetical civilization about to take its place; **Spiritus Mundi,** an alternative name for the *Anima Mundi*, or World Soul, which Yeats described as 'a general storehouse of images which have ceased to be a property of any personality or spirit'; **twenty centuries,** roughly the period since the birth of Christ.

p. 40 A Prayer for my Daughter: **Daughter,** Anne Yeats, born in Dublin on 26 February 1919; **Gregory's wood,** the poem was written at Thoor Ballylee, close to the woods of Coole; **trouble from a fool,** presumably Paris, whose elopement with Helen, wife of Menelaus, provoked the Trojan War; **great Queen,** Aphrodite, the Greek goddess of Love, born of the sea, and so fatherless; **bandy-leggèd smith,** Hephaestos, the lame smith and armour-maker to the gods, and Aphrodite's betrayed husband; **Horn of Plenty,** a cornucopia, overflowing with nectar and ambrosia, given to Zeus by the goat Amalthea; **a glad kindness,** celebrates Yeats's relationship with his wife; **loveliest woman,** Maud Gonne. **p. 42 Sailing to Byzantium**: **no country,** Ireland; **Byzantium,** capital of the Eastern Roman Empire, now Istanbul. Yeats thought that in its early days (and particularly in the reign of Justinian, 527–65) Byzantium had achieved Unity of Being so that 'religious, aesthetic and practical life were one, that architect and artificers . . . spoke to the multitude and the few alike'; **perne in a gyre,** to perne is to turn, and for 'gyre' see above. Yeats is asking the sages of Byzantium to gather him into their supernatural dimension by reversing the normal processes of history; **such a form,** Yeats had 'read somewhere that in the Emperor's palace at Byzantium was a tree made of gold and silver, and artificial birds that sang'. **p. 44 The Tower**: **Ben Bulben,** see above; **Plato and Plotinus,** Greek idealist and transcendental philosophers. Elsewhere Yeats admires them, but here they stand for the claims of the soul over the heart, and are repudiated in the final part of the poem; **Mrs. French,** like others mentioned in the poem, associated with the district which Yeats is viewing from the Ballylee battlements: she lived at Peterswell, and the incident of the ears is recorded in Jonah Barrington's *Recollections* (1827, 1832); **peasant girl,** Mary Hynes, a local beauty of the early C19th; **commended by a song,** the blind Gaelic poet Anthony Raftery (*c.* 1784–1835) wrote a poem in her praise; **Certain men,** Yeats took this incident from local folklore; **Homer,** like Raftery, the Greek poet Homer was blind and also celebrated a beautiful woman; **Hanrahan,** an imaginary character, a hedge schoolmaster who turns poet after being driven wild by his love for a goddess, and whose adventures are recounted in seven of Yeats's short stories; **old bawn,** probably a persistently uncorrected error for 'barn' where the incident takes place in Yeats's story. A bawn is a fortified mound; **old man's juggleries,** in Yeats's story 'Red Hanrahan' (the plot of which is retold in lines 57–73), Hanrahan is delayed from joining his sweetheart by a card-game with a mysterious stranger, who produces a hare and a pack of hounds from the cards; **forgotten what,** following the hounds, Hanrahan arrives at a house where a beautiful woman sits, tired with waiting. Too timid to question her or her companions, he lets his opportunity slip and awakes in the open air with his wits astray; **a man,** an early C19th bankrupt owner of the Tower, who could only venture out on Sundays because of his creditors; **centuries,** the Tower, originally one of the forts of the de Burgo family, went back to at least 1350; **Great Memory,** the *Anima Mundi* (see above); **wooden dice,** Yeats reported that 'ghosts have been seen at their game of dice in what is now my bedroom; **half-mounted man,** the bankrupt; **blind rambling celebrant,** Raftery; **red man,** Hanrahan; **country wench,** Mary Hynes; **Burke and Grattan,** two C18th Irish statesmen who championed national confidence and independence. Edmund Burke (1729–97), orator, politician, and writer supported the Irish Parliament and Catholic Emancipation and opposed Jacobinism and the French Revolution. The Irish politician and orator Henry Grattan (1746–1820) demanded legislative independence for Ireland and opposed the Union; **fabulous horn,** the cornucopia (see above); **make my soul,** prepare the soul for death.

p. 49 *Medititations in Time of Civil War*: The Irish Civil War broke out early in 1922 when a large minority of the Irish Parliament refused to accept the Anglo-Irish Treaty, and fighting continued into the following year; **Juno,** the Queen of the Gods in Roman mythology; **Il Penseroso's Platonist,** in John Milton's poem 'Il Penseroso' (1632) the poet asks 'let my Lamp at midnight hour, / Be seen in some high lonely Tow'r, / Where I may oft outwatch the *Bear,* / With thrice great *Hermes,* or unsphere/ The spirit of *Plato*; **Sato's gift,** a Japanese sword presented to Yeats by Junzo Sato, a Japanese postgraduate student, in Portland, Oregon, in 1920; **Chaucer,** The English poet Geoffrey Chaucer (c. 1345–1400) had in fact drawn breath; **Juno's peacock,** the peacock was sacred to Juno, and in *A Vision* a peacock's scream heralds a new historical cycle; **a woman and a man,** Yeats's 'bodily heirs', Anne and Michael Yeats; **Primum Mobile,** the primary source of movement in the Ptolemaic astronomical system; **old neighbour,** Lady Gregory; **a girl,** Yeats's wife, George Yeats; **affable irregular,** a member of the anti-Treaty Irish Republican Army; **Falstaffian,** like Sir John Falstaff, a fat, comic and affable Shakespearean character; **brown Lieutenant,** a member of the pro-Treaty Free State army; **stare,** starling; **Jacques Molay,** Grand Master of the Knights Templars, burned at the stake for heresy in Paris in 1314. Yeats, who regarded the Templars as forerunners of the French Revolution and Bolshevism, wrote that a 'cry for vengeance because of the murder of the Grand Master of the Templars seems to me fit symbol for those who labour for hatred, and so for sterility in various kinds'; **unicorns,** Yeats is thinking of *Ladies and Unicorns*, a painting by the French symbolist painter Gustave Moreau (1825–99); **Babylonian almanacs,** Babylon, the capital of ancient Mesopotamia, was famous for astronomy and astrology; **brazen hawks,** Yeats explained that the hawks were suggested by a ring of his 'with a hawk and a butterfly upon it, to symbolise the straight road of logic, and so of mechanism, and the crooked road of intuition: "For wisdom is a butterfly and not a gloomy bird of prey"'. **p. 55** *Leda and the Swan,* in Greek myth Zeus in the form of a swan raped Leda, wife of the King of Sparta, after seeing her bathing in the river Eurotas. From this union the twins Castor and Pollux were born, and also Helen, who was to cause the destruction of Troy; **Agamemnon dead,** Agamemnon commanded the Greek expedition to Troy to recover Helen, the errant wife of his brother Menelaus. On his return to Argos he was murdered by his wife Clytaemnestra (also a daughter of Leda) and her lover Aegisthus; **his knowledge with his power,** the rape of Leda by Zeus heralded a new civilization, and the poem questions how far humanity is the witting or unwitting agency of such apocalyptic change. **p. 56** *Among School Children*: occasioned by a visit Yeats made as a Senator in 1926 to St. Otteran's School, Waterford, which was run on Montessori principles; **Ledean body,** see above; **Plato's parable,** Plato's *Symposium* suggests that man was originally a self-sufficient egg-like sphere until Zeus divided him in two, and that love is the attempt of the halves to find their original unity; **she,** Maud Gonne; **daughters of the swan,** those, like Helen of Troy, who inherit the beauty and power of Leda and Zeus (see above); **Quattrocento,** an artist of the Italian fifteenth century; **Honey of generation,** sexual pleasure, sweet as honey, entices and betrays pre-natal souls into physicality. Yeats took the image from Prophyry's 'The Cave of the Nymphs'; **Plato thought,** Plato considered the physical world an imperfect copy of a world of Ideal Forms; **paradigm,** a pattern, is used by the Platonist Thomas Taylor to denote an archetype; **Solider Aristotle,** Aristotle (384–322 BC), a dissenting pupil of Plato, was 'solider' in believing that essential form must be identified with substance; **played the taws,** a taws is a leather strap, or a birch rod, used to punish disobedient pupils. Aristotle was the tutor of Alexander the Great ('king of kings'); **Pythagoras,** a Greek philosopher and mathematician, who flourished in the sixth century BC, believed that numbers and the ratios between numbers were the secret of harmony and beauty in music and the plastic arts. The epithet 'golden-thighed' was applied to him in classical times. **p. 58** *All Soul's Night*: **Christ Church bell,** 'Great Tom', the bell of Christ Church College, Oxford (the poem was written in Oxford); **All Souls' Night,** 2 November, when Catholics pray for the souls of the dead;

muscatel, strong sweet white wine; **Horton,** William Thomas Horton (1864–1919) a painter, mystic, and eccentric; **his lady,** Audrey Locke (1881–1916), with whom Horton lived platonically from 1914; **Anodyne,** pain-killing drug; **Emery,** Florence Farr Emery (1869–1917), an actress and ex-lover of Yeats, who helped with his experiments in chanting verse; **a school,** Ramanathan College in Ceylon, where she taught from 1912; **Mathers,** MacGregor Mathers (1854–1918), an occultist and co-founder of the Golden Dawn, whom Yeats had met in the late 1880s; **late estranged,** Yeats and the London Temple of the Golden Dawn had rebelled against Mathers' dictatorial leadership in 1900. **p. 61** *In Memory of Eva Gore-Booth . . . :* **Lissadell,** a late Georgian house, home to the Gore-Booths (see above); **gazelle,** a graceful small antelope, characterizing Eva (1870–1926), whom Yeats had thought of marrying in 1894, and who devoted her life to the suffragette movement and to working among Manchester mill-girls; **The older,** Constance Markiewicz (see above); **lonely days,** her husband and son left her to return to Poland; **gazebo,** a structure built as a place of observation. **p. 62** *Death:* inspired by the assassination of Kevin O'Higgins (1892–1927), Irish Minister of Justice and a friend of Yeats. **p. 63** *A Dialogue of Self and Soul:* **winding ancient stair,** that in the Tower at Ballylee (see above); **Montashigi,** in fact Bushü Osafuné Motoshigé, who flourished in the era of Oei (1394–1428). **p. 65** *Coole and Ballylee, 1931:* **dark Raftery's cellar,** Raftery, 'dark' because blind (see above), described the hole where the river goes underground at Ballylee as 'a strong cellar'; **generated soul,** in Neoplatonic tradition water generates images in the mind; **buskin,** a high boot worn by tragic actors in ancient Greece; **somebody,** Lady Gregory; **last inheritor,** Lady Gregory, because Coole had been sold and would not pass to her grandson, Richard; **book of the people,** a phrase borrowed from Raftery. Yeats and Lady Gregory based much of their work on Irish folklore and myth; **high horse,** Pegasus (see above). **p. 67** *Swift's Epitaph:* a version of the Latin epitaph that the Irish writer, satirist, and clergyman Jonathan Swift (1667–1745) wrote for himself. **p. 67** *At Algeciras . . . :* Yeats was dangerously ill in November 1927 at Algeciras, southern Spain; **narrow straits,** the Pillars of Hercules which divide Europe from Africa and the Mediterranean from the Atlantic (hence 'mingled seas'); **Newton's metaphor:** the scientist and mathematician Sir Isaac Newton (1642–1727) compared his discoveries to a boy finding curious shells on a seashore while the 'great ocean of truth lay all undiscovered before me'; **Rosses,** see above; **the Great Questioner,** God in judgement. **p. 68** *Byzantium:* **night-walkers,** prostitutes; **dome,** of the Hagia

Sophia, a cathedral in Byzantium and now a mosque; **Hades' bobbin,** a mummy, imagined as a spindle on which life can be wound and rewound; **dolphin,** in Neoplatonic tradition dolphins carry the souls of the dead to the afterlife; **Marbles,** the Emperor's pavements of line 25, on which the spirits dance during purification. **p. 69** *Vacillation*: **A tree there is,** *The Mabinogion*, a compilation of Welsh mythology, describes a tree 'one half of which was in flames from the root to the top, and the other half was green and in full leaf'; **Attis,** a vegetation god associated with seasonal death and rebirth. His followers ritually castrated themselves, and hung his effigy on a sacred tree to ensure regeneration; **ram ... with sun,** from Ben Jonson's *Poetaster*, V i 136; **Lethean,** forgetful: Lethe was the river of oblivion in Greek myth; **lord of Chou,** Chou-Kung, a twelfth-century Chinese warlord; **Babylon or Nineveh,** capital cities of respectively, ancient Mesopotamia and Assyria; **Isaiah's coal,** in Isaiah 6: vi-vii an angel touches Isaiah's lips with a burning coal to purge his sins; **Von Hügel,** Baron Friedrich von Hügel (1852–1925), a Catholic theologian who, like Yeats, took mysticism and miracles seriously; **Saint Teresa,** a Spanish nun and visionary (1515–82), whose corpse was reputed to have remained uncorrupted; **self-same hands,** Yeats suggests that St. Teresa's body may have been embalmed by the ghosts of ancient Egyptian embalmers; **lion and the honeycomb,** see Judges 14:14, where Samson takes honey from bees nesting in a lion's carcass, so that 'from the strong came forth sweetness'. **p. 73** *Stream and Sun at Glendalough,* records an epiphanic moment at Glendalough, an important site of early Irish Christianity. **p. 74** *Crazy Jane Talks with the Bishop*: **excrement,** see Blake, *Jerusalem,* 88:39: 'I will make their places of joy & love, excrementious'. **p. 75** *Her Vision in the Wood*: **the beast,** the boar who killed Adonis, a beautiful youth loved by Aphrodite; **Quattrocento,** the fifteenth century, see above; **Mantegna,** Andrea Mantegna (1431–1506), Italian painter noted for the skill of his composition. **p. 76** *Meru*: a holy mountain in Tibet and a place of pilgrimage. **p. 77** *The Gyres*: **Old Rocky Face,** the Delphic Oracle; **Empedocles,** a Greek philosopher, (*c.* 493–*c.* 433 BC), who taught that the world is composed of four elements – air, fire, earth, and water – which interact under the influence of two cosmic powers, Love and Strife, so that the universe is perpetually oscillating between the poles of unity and diversity; **Hector,** Trojan hero, son of Priam and Hecuba, whose death at the hands of Achilles hastened the sack and burning ('light') of Troy; **tragic joy,** 'the creative joy of acceptance of what life brings', a concept Yeats derived from the German philosopher Friedrich Nietzsche. **p. 78** *Lapis Lazuli*: **Clifton,** Henry (Harry) Clifton gave the carved piece of lapis lazuli (blue silicate) to Yeats as a 70th birthday present; **Zeppelin,** German airships which had bombed London in the First World War; **King Billy,** William of Orange (William III), who had defeated James II's Irish forces at the Battle of the Boyne (see above). Yeats borrows 'bomb balls' from a popular ballad on the subject; **drop scenes,** curtains dropped between the audience and the stage at the end of a play; **Callimachus,** Greek sculptor who flourished in the late 5th century BC, and was said to have designed a bronze lamp, shaped like a palm, for the Erechtheum on the Acropolis. **p. 79** *An Acre of Grass*: **old house,** Riversdale in the Dublin suburb of Rathfarnham, Yeats's last home; **Timon and Lear,** Shakespearean tragic heroes, who in old age are forced to a passionate re-evaluation of all that they are; **Blake,** William Blake (1757–1827), poet and engraver, who kept his imaginative energy to his death. **p. 81** *The Curse of Cromwell*: Oliver Cromwell (1599–1658) commanded the anti-Royalist forces in the English Civil War and became Lord Protector after the execution of Charles I. His military campaign in Ireland was notorious for massacre, destruction and dispossession; **the Spartan boy's,** Plutarch relates that a Spartan boy hid a stolen fox under his clothes and let it gnaw him to death rather than disclose his theft. **p. 82** *Why should not Old Men be Mad?*: **all Dante once,** Iseult Gonne; **dunce,** Iseult's husband, the Irish novelist Francis Stuart; **Helen of social welfare,** Maud Gonne. **p. 82** *The Statues*: **Pythagoras,** see above; **Greater than Pythagoras:** Yeats suggests that Greek sculptors were even more influential than the mathematicians in translating abstract equations into physical form; **Asiatic vague immensities,** Yeats commented that 'the arts must once again accept those Greek proportions which carry into plastic art the Pythagorean numbers, those faces which are divine because all there is empty and measured. Europe was not born when Greek galleys defeated the Persian hordes at Salamis; but when the Doric studios sent out those broad-backed marble statues against the multiform, vague, expressive Asiatic sea, they gave to the sexual instinct of Europe its goal, its fixed type'; **Salamis,** the sea battle of Salamis in 480BC, at which the Greeks defeated a superior Persian fleet, was one of the decisive battles of the world; **Phidias,** see above; **one image,** the armies of Alexander the Great carried the Greek idea of proportion into upper India where, in statues of Buddha, it grew rounded and less precise and athletic; **Hamlet thin with eating flies,** Shakespeare's Hamlet represented as a gaunt thinker, undernourished by abstract thought; **Dreamer of the Middle Ages,** Yeats used this phrase of the English poet William Morris (1834–96), whose broad body 'yet half remembers Buddha's motionless meditation, and has no trait in common with the wavering, lean image of hungry speculation, that cannot but because of certain famous Hamlets of our stage fill the mind's eye'; **Grimalkin,** a witch's cat (see Macbeth I i 8); **Pearse summoned Cuchulain,** Pearse (see above) made a cult of the ancient Irish hero Cuchulain (see above); **Post Office,** centre of fighting during the 1916 Rising. **p. 84** *Long-legged Fly*: **Caesar,** Julius Caesar (102–44 BC), the Roman commander and strategist, but here standing for any engrossed man of action; **topless towers . . . She,** Troy and Helen, echoing Marlowe's description in *Dr. Faustus* (1604) V i; **first Adam,** Michelangelo's painting on the Sistine Chapel ceiling of Adam being brought to life by God. **p. 85** *A Bronze Head*: inspired by a bronze-painted plaster-cast by Laurence Campbell in the Municipal Gallery, Dublin; **tomb-haunter,** Maud Gonne habitually wore black in old age; **Hysterico Passio,** passionate hysteria, from *King Lear* II iv; **McTaggart,** J.M.E. McTaggart (1866–1925) a Cambridge Hegelian philosopher. **p. 86** *Man and the Echo*: **Alt,** a glen on Knocknarea, a mountain near Sligo; **that play,** *Cathleen ni Houlihan* (1902), a one-act play in which a woman, personifying Ireland, incites a young bridegroom to armed rebellion and death; **certain men,** the leaders of 1916; **that woman,** the actress Margot Ruddock (Collis), with whom Yeats had an affair and whom he and his wife helped when she went mad in Barcelona; **a house,** Coole Park, demolished by the Irish Forestry Commission; **bodkin,** a dagger, associated through *Hamlet*, III i with suicide. **p. 88** *The Circus Animals' Desertion*: **circus animals,** Yeats's works and poetical resources; **sea-rider Oisin,** in Yeats's first substantial poem, 'The Wanderings of Oisin', the hero is taken by Niamh (see above) to three islands representing infinite sensuality, infinite battle and infinite repose, but finds lasting contentment in none of them; **counter-truth,** Oisin leaves the real world for fairyland, in **The Countess Cathleen** (1892) the heroine, based on Maud Gonne, rejects the attractions of the imagination for intervention in the world, selling her soul to feed her famine-stricken tenants; **the Fool and the Blindman,** characters in *On Baile's Strand* (1903) who parody the heroes of the play, Cuchulain and Conchubar, in their representation of strength and guile; **ungovernable sea,** after killing his son, Cuchulain is enchanted into expending his fury on the incoming tide (see above); **raving slut,** a Muse figure; in an early draft Yeats described 'that raving slut / Called Heart and Company'.